DIRECT HIT

A BOLD TAKE ON INTERNATIONAL CRICKET..

VENKAT BALANTRAPU

Made with ♥ on the Notion Press Platform
www.notionpress.com

“DIRECT HIT”

(A BOLD TAKE ON INTERNATIONAL CRICKET)

Contents

Contents

Contents

Foreword

DIRECT HIT

Venkat Balantrapu has been an insurance professional for over 38 years.He began his insurance career as a Class I Officer in the year 1986 with one of the public sector insurers in India. After serving in India for 12 years, he took up senior overseas assignments in the insurance sector in 1998 immediately on being promoted to the rank of a Divisional Manager. This lit his career path and enabled him hold very senior positions, heading the entire operations of insurance companies as well as heading the insurance companies in Kenya, Mauritius, Uganda, Tanzania, Zambia and Malawi as well for over two decades.

He is an ex-banker too and has worked in the private sector as well for 5 years. Though he never eyed an insurance career initially, he grabbed the opportunity, a life changing moment, to become a successful and time tested senior global insurance professional.

Born and brought up in Chennai, India, he is currently based in Mauritius as the COO of IOGA Ltd, a general insurance firm there. He is also pursuing his passion of transformational coaching and speaking vigorously and is a Certified Leadership & Career Mastery Coach and a Customer Retention Strategist, helping people in their career growth. He has been enabling people from all walks of life to realize their true and immense potential as well as overcome their biggest obstacles in life with a view to enabling them become their best version, something they either always dreamt of or never dared to even dream about...!

He is a published author and poet and a columnist, writing on leadership, management, career transformation and international cricket. He has played competitive cricket in India and the African continent for over 3 decades. An avid Golfer, he actively competes in Carrom and Table Tennis competitions as well and is a passionate singer.

Preface

PREFACE

The reason this book is titled **"DIRECT HIT"** is to share through this book, whatever I have observed, analysed, felt about and wrote without any inhibition on the happenings in international cricket all around, for over a decade and a half, focusing equally on international teams as well as international cricketers. I have, thro this book, taken out some excerpts of my writings on various global platforms which include my weekly articles in The Independent(a Mauritus based english daily), Sports Monthly(a Kenya based monthly sports magazine) and various websites viz., www.msn.co.in; www.cricjoy.com; www.thecricketblog.com and www.thecricketcountry.com for a long period.

This book is my sincere attempt to share my bold take on the happenings in international cricket and how the game has evolved over the last decade post the first T20 world cup in 2007, the emergence of popular world T20 leagues(starting with the much followed cricket spectacle, the IPL), the 2011 world cup and culminating with the 2013 champions trophy.

This is the period of transition post the millenium for the game of cricket as a whole when many a career were made, budding cricketers became international starts and international stars faded away slowly, thanks to the advent of the shortest format of the game as well as age catching up with them and their reflexes. But as they say, form is temporary and class is permanent, most of these stars did exit gracefully by showing a glimpse of their class even in the shortest and fiercely competitive format.

This book encompasses each of the three formats, Test Cricket, ODI's and T20's in equal proportions and it not only throws light on how the game evolved and fared during this period, but offers interesting facts, tales and exciting moments on the game, cricket playing nations, cricketing stars, international tournaments including tri-nations cups or cricketing series betwen nations, offering minute coverage of rare insights into team as well as individual records achieved, broken and missed out narrowly.

I strongly believe this book will offer an opportunity to current and former cricket stars to relive some of their career's best moments, cricket playing countries to look back as to how they fared in the long run, budding cricketers to take a leaf out of former cricketers and understand the fine line between becoming an international cricket star and just being an also ran in international cricket. The biggest takeaway from this book will be understanding what it takes to reach the top and stay there thro sheer endurance. As they say, "the tough get going when the going gets tough" - a story of those who have left a legacy in cricket.

A quick read of this book offers exciting moments from weekly round-ups on happenings in international cricket as well as from specific games. This book offers you a very flexible and convenient read as you can pick and choose any of the chapters or any of the periods in which matches were played without worrying about losing the continuity in your reading.

This book is "A Bold Take On International Cricket"....!

Acknowledgements

I thank...........
My wife, Jayalalitha Balantrapu
My daughter, Apoorva Balantrapu
My daughter, Sai Akshara Balantrapu
For standing by me throughout my challenges
And their understanding and support throughout my journey.
I dedicate this book of mine
to my late father,
a leading journalist and a footballer himself,
for always encouraging
the sportsman in me
before eventually inspiring
me to becoming both
an author as well as a columnist.

Prologue

CHAPTER ONE

KOHLINOOR OF INDIAN CRICKET

He came, he saw and he conquered the hearts of millions of Indian cricket fans. This is the story of Virat Kohli the shining star of Indian cricket.

Immediately after leading India to the U-19 World Cup victory, Kohli got a call to play for the senior Indians. It's measure of this confidence and maturity that he proved himself worthy in a team of heavyweights. He came in as stop-gap for the injured Virender Sehwag in 2008 and grabbed his chances to raise hope as India's principal hope to take the batting mantle from the ageing seniors.

Rarely has he failed to justify his place in Team India's playing XI. At times when players like Sachin Tendulkar, Sehwag and Gautam Gambhir were unavailable, Kohli has held the fort with supreme confidence. He is one batsman who has convincingly carried his recent form not only into the warm-up matches, but also into the world cup match. Along with Sehwag, Kohli's unbeaten century avenged India's 2007 loss to Bangladesh.

Kohli was hardly one year old when Tendulkar made his debut for India. Today, he stands tall alongside the maestro when it comes to the expectations of the fans. Kohli's solidity gives confidence to Sehwag, Tendulkar and Yuvraj Singh to play attacking cricket in case of early fall of wickets and enable guys like Mahendra Singh Dhoni and Yusuf Pathan to create mayhem at the death.

In Kohli, India has a cool and level headed frontline batsman who knows how to preserve his wicket under any situation. His maturity beyond his young age indicates he is India's future Mr. Wall.

India has undoubtedly found a future star in him who seems to have understood the language of taming different attacks in different conditions. The day is not far when the India's "Fab Four" will not be around. But in Kohli, India is fortunate to have the first quality replacement in place.

Credit should go to Dhoni who has seen the rising star in Kohli, similar to Sourav Ganguly grooming today's stars like Yuvraj, Zaheer Khan and Harbhajan in their formative years. Dhoni backed Kohli for the No. 4 slot and the result is a spectacular century on debut in the world cup.

Kohli has won the confidence of his captain by consistently proving his credential right through 2010. Bailing out Delhi from a precarious situation in 2005, leading India to U-19 World Cup triumph in 2008 and cementing his place in the playing XI for India through consistent performances are only the initial steps of a promising career ahead. In him, India has a future captain as well, certainly for all the formats.

He is the fastest Indian to aggregate 1,000 runs in ODI's. Being ranked 13th, behind three other Indians in October, 2010, Kohli has now jumped to 2nd place in ICC ODIrankings, leaving all the three senior Indian batsmen behind him.

This ranking was prior to his hundred against Bangladesh. These are clear testimony to his commitment and unrivalled batting abilities at such a young age. He has not only given the much-needed stability to the batting line-up, but has also enabled Team India hold its head high!

The Kohinoor is very much in India. It's renamed "Kohlinoor".

CHAPTER TWO

AUSTRALIA LOOKS A TEAM SANS STEAM

(Week ending March 09, 2013)

After losing the ODI series 1-2 to England, hosts Kiwis have begun the 3 Test series with a bang. Inspite of the first day's play being washed out, New Zealand have gained an upper hand on day two. The visitors, touted as a very good side and fresh from drubbing India on their backyard, were skittled out for only 167. The hosts, thanks to their openers, are on the verge of taking a massive lead. It is almost certain the hosts will emerge with a 1-0 lead from the Dunedin Test.

Debutant Neil Wagner stole the day with a double blow in the first over of the match to miss a hat-trick very narrowly. Another debutant at 32, Bruce Martin, shared the honours with Wagner with each of the claiming 4 wickets apiece. This 167 is England's lowest first innings total since 2009 and for New Zealand, this first wicket partnership above 131 was last achieved way back in 2004, incidentally against the same team.

Pakistan, after a T20 win against South Africa, will take on the hosts in a five match ODI series. With seniors like Shahid Afridi, Shoaib Malik, Umar Akmal and Kamran Akmal back in the squad, the visitors are sure to increase their chances of an upset series win. With Wahab Riaz also back, their bowling arsenal looks further strengthened. South Africa will have their hands full in coping with bowlers like Saeed Ajmal, Junaid Khan and Umar Gul in this short version. Since five matches will be played, any initial lapses by either team can be overcome with a strategic game cum series plan.

With the axing of Virender Sehwag for the remaining two Tests, India have sent a clear message to it's players to either perform or perish, irrespective of past laurels. For Sehwag, it was sooner than later looking into his dismal form in more than 25 innings with his batting average tottering in the 20's. Australia, instead of improving their show, put up one of their worst ever performances to succumb to India in Hyderabad early on the

4th day. With this win, Dhoni became the Indian captain with most Test wins surpassing Sourav Ganguly's 8 year old record. This result also made Michael Clarke the first captain ever to lose a Test by an innings after declaring the first innings, batting first.

Almost every Indian player has struck form in this series. The lack of form of the remaining has not mattered. Their bowlers' inability on Indian wickets and the absence of Ponting and Hussey are hurting Australia . This team, excepting Clarke cannot handle spin, but are putting their team in a spin!

CHAPTER THREE

BANGLA TIGERS FINALLY TAMED

(Week ending March 24, 2012)

International cricket was witness to two of the game's biggest achievements last week, viz., Sachin Tendulkar's 100th hundred and Bangladesh making it to the Asia Cup finals, their first of any major cricketing event. The first one may never see a repeat in international cricket, especially with the rampant reduction in no. of Tests being played and the emergence of too many T20 matches. The second one was bound to happen sooner or later looking at the giant strides the Bangladeshis have made in the recent past by way of increase in the quality of cricket they have been playing. The week was also witness to Sri Lanka's slide to the bottom of the Asia Cup points table for the first time, that too by losing all the matches in the league phase, also for the first time. Only a week ago, the Lankans showed us glimpses of their high calibre cricket when they rightfully played the CB Series finals and it is a surprise the magic has vanished in thin air during the Asia Cup.

Tendulkar's landmark hundred was finally achieved in the match against Bangladesh. Better late than never and as admitted by himself, it was his toughest 100 in his career. It might have come against a team which people perceive as relatively easy. But the fact will remain he did it and did it after scoring 99 centuries before this. The magic of this elusive century is such that everyone was focussed on this and not the earlier 99 centuries. Full credit to Tendulkar for having withstood the pressures of international cricket for 23 years and still remaining unscathed and if anyone could achieve it, it was meant to be only him and none deserved it better than him. Though he has achieved everything in cricket, his continued passion will make it impossible for anyone to match his achievements.

It was a case of so near yet so far for Bangladesh to lose the Asia Cup finals by 2 runs when they let Pakistan off the hook and gifted them the Asia Cup. Inability to hit even one boundary in the last 18 balls with wickets in hand ensured Bangladesh's dream of a historic Asia Cup remained a dream. Instead of the cup, they won the hearts of millions of cricket fans by their daredevilry. Reaching the finals, that too by beating India and Sri Lanka will remain their biggest cricketing achievement till date. With this performance, they have earned immense respect and a lot of self-belief and confidence.

Down west, Australia's tour of the Windies has begun with the 5 match ODI series on expected lines. It is currently poised on 1-1 after 3 matches with the third ending on a scintillating tie, which otherwise had a win written for the Windies, but for the needless run out with two balls to spare. These are the incidents which make an ODI very interesting and unpredictable. But the notable aspect of this series so far is that the Windies broke the jinx of not beating the Aussies in an ODI for 6 years when they won the second ODI, after 13 consecutive losses. From the Aussies side, it took them three matches for any of their batsmen to score the first half century of the series. Looking into the way the series has progressed so far and the prevailing pitch and ground conditions, it looks highly unlikely unlike the Asia Cup that any team will be able to score in excess of 300. The series is being closely fought and it will not be a cake walk for the Aussies and if they need to win the series, they need to sweat it out, but with no guarantee. The Windies, having replaced Kieran Powell with Adrian Barath, just recovered from a finger injury, for the last 2 ODI's, will keep their fingers crossed hoping for a series win.

Having lost the T20 and the ODI series respectively, the ongoing third Test is the last chance for New Zealand to restore some pride. A failure here will ensure they succumb to the Test series as well as they are already trailing 0-1, having lost the second Test. If they win this Test and level the series, they will reaffirm their fine show earlier this year when they squared a series in Australia and whitewashed Zimbabwe at home. For South Africa, if they either win or draw this Test, they will end up wrapping all the three formats and this will be one of their biggest tour wins. This will also keep them in a good stead and boost their confidence in their respective fixtures against the Aussies and England later this year. Most importantly, they will be taking a well deserved step closer to the no.1 Test ranking.

CHAPTER FOUR

BATTLE FOR THE FINAL FRONTIER BEGINS

(Week ending February 23, 2013)

India take on Australia in a four match Test series, the much awaited one of 2013. For India, this will be a perfect platform to restore lost pride after their dismal Test record in the recent past. They have undoubtedly let down their fans and have fallen a few notches lower in their fans' eyes. Added to this, is the current controversial phase of their master blaster Tendulkar's career. Vis-à-vis his own standards and other international cricketers, including his colleagues in Team India, his form has taken a hitherto unseen low dip. Under the circumstances, it is extremely difficult to justify his place in the playing eleven. Personally for him, this series will be the biggest test of his career. Irrespective of whether he succeeds here or fails yet again, this series, in all likelihood, will be his last against Australia. Emerging winners in a India-Australia series is the ultimate to either team.

Australia, surprisingly, announced their playing XI for the first Test a few days in advance whilst India had to grapple with two issues concerning team composition. One issue is choosing Sehwag's opening partner and the other is to get their bowling combination right. In both cases, the team management is facing the dilemma of one too many. But it looks like Murali Vijay, being from Chennai as well as a senior, will get a nod ahead of Shikar Dhawan and Harbhajan will make it to the playing XI purely due to his past performance against the Aussies and the presence of many left handers in their current team. For Australia, Shane Watson will bat at no.4 in a team with four pacers and Nathan Lyon as the lone spinner. Based on his warm-up games performance, debutant Henriques has pipped Glenn Maxwell for a place in the XI. The main concern for Australia will be that their skipper Michael Clarke as well as opener David Warner are coming from injuries and only time will tell how well they have recovered. Both teams are in a transition phase and it is to be seen who will cope with the pressure better. With a couple of senior batsmen each from either team retiring recently, the teams are evenly placed but the home conditions and spin friendly tracks are bound to help India win the series unless they repeat the tactical errors committed against England under similar conditions.

England and New Zealand go into the final ODI with the series tied at 1-1. The Kiwis won the first match and the English, the second. The captains played a crucial part in their respective wins. After losing the first match, England romped home in the second, aided by a superb five-wicket haul by Jimmy Anderson. This was supported by almost all their frontline batsmen chipping in with useful contributions to ensure a successful run chase inspite of Brendon McCullum's blitzkrieg and former skipper Ross Taylor's comeback hundred for New Zealand. It is pathetic that McCullum's strike rate of 205.55 ended in a losing cause.

After getting thoroughly mauled at Wanderers and Newlands to succumb to a 0-2 series loss, Pakistan will go into the third Test with nothing more to lose but warm up for the forthcoming ODI. It is sad to note a talented team playing the final Test only for academic interest.

CHAPTER FIVE

BCCI HAS IT'S WAY YET AGAIN

(Week ending June 30, 2012)

A confident England will play Australia in 5 ODI's hoping to continue their winning spree. Only few days back, have England drubbed West Indies, yet again showing the world they are a tough nut to crack while playing at home. While England are confidence personified, the Aussies can prove dangerous, especially having picked quite a few youngsters who are proving to be proven performers.

For England, Ian Bell and Alistair Cook are the men in form coming into this series with brilliant centuries against the West Indies. Their middle order too is strengthened by the presence of men like Ravi Bopara, Johny Bairstow, Jonathan Trott and Eoin Morgan. It goes without saying that England has the most potent bowling combination in international cricket as on date. James Anderson, Stuart Broad and Tim Bresnan are becoming bowlers who will always excel whilst their offie Graeme Swann is undoubtedly the smartest spinner around.

For Australia, the absence of Ricky Ponting and Michael Hussey should not dent their chances as their formidable opening pair of Shane Watson and David Warner are ably backed by David Hussey, Peter Forrest, Steve Smith and George Bailey. With Ben Hilfenhaus, Pat Cummins and James Pattinson around coupled with the likely return of Mitchell Johnson, the series is set to see a keen tussle between the bowlers of both sides.

In another international series to be played between New Zealand and West Indies, the Kiwis will play their hosts in a long series comprising of 2 T20's, 5 ODI's and 2 Tests. For a change the T20's are set to be played in Lauderhill, Florida, USA with a view to promoting the game there. With players like Darren Bravo, Tino Best and Andre Russell not picked, most of them due to injuries, the West indies have picked uncapped leg spinner Samuel Badree for the T20's. The team is focused on the forthcoming T20 world cup and their priority is to find the best combination and keep them fit and in form for the mega event. On completion of the T20's the teams are set to return to the Caribbean to play the remaining formats.

The Decision Review System is set to haunt the ICC yet again. Inspite of the Executive Board deciding to unilaterally implement the DRS, the BCCI has stuck to it's guns. This has resulted in the ICC yet again deciding against making the use of DRS mandatory. After a bitter experience in the 2008 series against Sri Lanka, India had always opposed the use of the DRS. India is not averse to the idea of supporting this, provided it is 100% error free.

Technology introduction has always been controversial, but slowly and surely, teams have been accepting the use of DRS. On one hand , enough controversy has been generated by using this technology as many a time, decisions have been flawed. On the other, looking at the level, pattern and extent of errors international umpires have been making, one is made to believe the only way out to make decisions reasonably accurate is by the use of technology.

Mr. Harron Lorgat and Mr. Sharad Pawar are set to be replaced by Dave Richardson and Mr. Alan Isaac respectively. Let us hope these new men at the helm of affairs rid the game of controversies!

CHAPTER SIX

CENTURIES GALORE DURING THE WEEK

(Week ending November 15, 2012)

Three Tests during the week, two of them incomplete, have produced 12 centuries including two double centuries so far. Only the Australia-South Africa Test has petered into a tame draw, thanks to the third day being completely washed out. At the end of their innings and after making early inroads into the Aussie innings, the Proteas seemed to be on a roll. But Australian skipper Michael Clarke, a man in sublime form, stepped in with his own script and rewrote the rest of the Test.

Clarke's 259 not out is nothing less than an incredible feat. Not just because it is a double ton, but because it is his third and all of them have come in 2012. This one has a special mark on it as he steered his team out of trouble to safety, built a healthy lead and went on to put the visitors in a precarious position when they batted second time. While Clarke's teammate Ed Cowan got his maiden hundred and Mike Hussey added one more, the Test began with the two best South African batsmen Jacques Kallis and Hashim Amla scoring a ton apiece earlier. Kallis has now scored 44 Test hundreds and is not far behind Sachin Tendulkar.

Two Tests are now being played in the sub-continent. West Indies' first innings is a repeat story of the Aussies' innings against South Africa. The Windies too lost three early wickets and it looked like the hosts Bangladesh have come of age in Test cricket. The visitors' man Friday, Shivnaraine Chanderpaul, the most hungry batsman in Test cricket today rescued his team with the help of Dinesh Ramdin, thanks to a record stand. Bangladesh could not dislodge this partnership and had to wait for the rival skipper to declare at 527 for 4 with Chanderpaul reaching the second double ton of his career equalling his previous best with an unbeaten 203.

While Powell and Dinesh Ramdin rallied around Chanderpaul with a century each, it was Tamim Iqbal who was the cynosure of all eyes when he scored a whirlwind 72 spraying boundaries all over. However, once he vanished with an irresponsible shot, it was Naeem Islam who restored some pride in the hosts' batting with a patient knock of 108. These two innings, alongwith other useful contributions including Shakib Al Hassan's 89, ensured Bangladesh did not have to follow on in front of their home crowd.

Back in India, Virender Sehwag silenced his critics with a bang. With an opening stand of 134, Sehwag went on to make 117, his 23rd Test hundred. His last Test ton came in 2010. With this, he became the second batsman to score 6 of his hundreds with a strike rate of over 100 which includes 3 double centuries. Only Adam Gilchrist has done it 7 times and it is a matter of time before Sehwag does it again. Inspite of international hundreds flying all around, it is unfortunate, Sachin Tendulkar, the man with the highest centuries to his credit failed yet again to reach the landmark, his last coming in January 2011.

England's Graeme Swann overtook Jim Laker as their most successful spinner when he bowled Sehwag. Incidentally, Swann's wickets riot has come in a week where no other bowler has managed a five wicket haul!

CHAPTER SEVEN

LEGEND LAXMAN CALLS IT A DAY

(Week ending August 18, 2012)

Ever since India won the world cup last year, they have taken a back seat in Test cricket. Following the 8 consecutive overseas defeats, they have slipped down the rankings and have lost two of their most prominent and irreplaceable batsmen. While Dravid retired some time back, Laxman's sudden retirement, especially after being picked to play the Kiwis at home is unexplained and has surprised one and all. With Tendulkar too not expected to carry on for a long time, the biggest test for India in the coming years will be to fill the void created by the end of the golden batting era for India. Forced to select youngsters, India might struggle to get their batting order right in the upcoming Test series against New Zealand.

Having made his Test debut for India in 1996, Laxman played 134 Tests and batted on 225 occasions and averaged 45.97. His 17 centuries may seem to be of no significance when one looks at the number, but the timing of each of them speaks volumes about this batting legend. Each of them are very very special in their own way. His highest score of 281 n.o against the mighty Aussies in Kolkata will always be cherished by every Indian fan and will also remain as one of the all-time great Test knocks. This innings enabled India to register a historic win, having followed on and also clinch the series inspite of trailing 0-1 which subsequently changed the face of Indian cricket forever.

His speciality has been setting his own pace for his innings, carrying on with the tail-enders and exhibiting wristy stroke play with a silken touch and surgical precision. He always ground the opposition into submission and has been a fourth innings specialist extremely difficult to deal with. Laxman's best knocks and most centuries came out against the best, the Aussies. His knocks against the Aussies, especially the Kolkata one and the century at Adelaide will be etched in our memories forever. At the crease, he was truly an artist at work.

In England, it looks like curtains down for Kevin Pietersen. Inspite of being one of the game's destructive batsmen, his divisive influence in the dressing room seems to have put an end to his stint with England. His absence in the Lord's Test coupled with the Proteas' domination throughout the series saw England concede the no.1 spot to the visitors. South Africa well and truly deserved this, especially after the hard work and efforts they put in during the last couple of years. Inspite of losing Boucher to a freak injury at the start of the series, they went on to achieve the improbable and will now happily dedicate this feat to him as he has always been a part of this dream team. It is not a surprise England lost the series 0-2 and the top spot, having lost 6 out of their last 11 Tests.

India and Australia have deservedly qualified to play the U19 world cup finals this Sunday. In the semis, the Aussies overcame the South Africans inspite of a fragile start in their chase whilst the Indians outclassed the Kiwis in a close encounter. Irrespective of who wins this cup, there are already a few future stars lined up!

CHAPTER EIGHT

AUSSIES NEED TO PULL OUT A HOUDINI'S ACT

(Week ending November 23, 2013)

It is not even three months since the Aussies were drubbed in an Ashes series and they are now ready to face the prospect of another Ashes drubbing, this time at home. Thanks to the world cup next year in Australia, they are required to handle the English onslaught yet again before the customary 18 months gap for an Ashes series.

There seems to be a huge gap in standards and form between the two players, especially looking into the Australians' repeated Ashes disappointments in the recent past and 0-4 rout received in the hands of the Indians in India recently. They may be playing at home in front of their supporters on wickets conducive to their bowling style. Added to this, Mitchell Johnson who was not picked for the previous Ashes in England is now back in the squad, thanks to injuries sustained by Mitchell Starc, Pattinson and Bird. But are these going to change their fortunes? The hosts will do well to remember they have not won a Test since January this year and the only team they have beaten in a Test since the last summer is Sri Lanka. Two major factors lacking in the Aussies of late have been their usual arrogant confidence and Test match temperament amongst the current bunch of new generation players.

The Gabba wicket, where only four of the Australians who played here last time against South Africa will be playing now, is renowned for its pace and bounce. With showers expected most of the match days this time around, the Aussie batsmen may find the conditions a bit too tricky to handle. With skipper Michael Clarke set to overcome his own injury woes, Australia can hope for their other batsmen to rally around him, especially after having received a shot in the arm with the inclusion of George Bailey. The Aussies last lost in the Gabba 25 years ago. With a long 5 Test battle ahead, this will be the perfect start for the hosts if they can come unscathed here.

If Bailey will bat at no.6 for Australia, England have made a clever move by roping in Michael Carberry which will mean Joe Root will fill the no.6 slot. Jonny Bairstow will keep for England if Matt Prior fails to recover in time. Alistair Cook, the thorn in the Aussies' flesh will remain so. This will be Kevin Pietersen's 100th Test and he sure will have his own plans. Right now, the Aussie bowling line-up doesn't look a threat to the English batsmen who look a well settled and well oiled unit.

On England's part, they can regain the no.2 Test spot from India who moved ahead with a 2-0 win over the Windies last week. If Australia regain the Ashes or even manage to draw this series, they will also come back into the top four in the rankings table by pushing back Pakistan. With Australia playing at home and their ever reliable skipper leading from the front with loads of runs, they can surely put behind the shambolic recent past.

The Ashes story took a sharp turn ever since 2005 with England winning four of the last five Ashes series which looked highly unlikely at the turn of the century. The visitors have won 8 of the last 15 Ashes Tests. With the previous coach fired and grappling with some disciplinary issues within the team during the previous Ashes series, time will tell if the Kangaroos will really bounce back though they look quite buoyant right now. Will the English be able to win a fourth consecutive Ashes now, having last done so in 1880? The Aussies have the answer and they need to be at their best to halt this. For this, they need to pull out a Houdini's act!

CHAPTER NINE

DEFLATED INDIA TAKE ON ELATED ENGLAND

(Week ending December 08, 2012)

When England landed in India, none gave them a chance to survive. The first Test went on expected lines, towards the fate in store for the Englishmen against the guile of Indian spin. However, when everything seemed to be going India's way midway in the second Test, the English spinners, led by Monty, spun the wheel of fortune in their favour, much more than the Indian spin trio spun the ball. By day four, it was very evident that Dhoni failed to capitalise on a turning pitch, unwarranted spin trio and the toss advantage, thereby tossing the match away on a platter to England, totally surprising them. Ofcourse, this would not have been possible but for the magnanimity shown by the Indian batsmen, not once, but twice in the match.

With the Mumbai loss, India's plans of total revenge have gone with the wind and they are now busy trying to salvage lost pride. India's clueless batting display at the Wankhede has shown how important the presence of Dravid, Laxman and Ganguly had been to the team in the recent past. It looks Cheteshwar Pujara is the only odd man out in the current batting line-up, thanks to his fine show, with the rest looking pathetic. To add insult to injury, the Indian bowling seems to be at their lowest ebb and their skipper is struggling to be amongst runs.

India need to put the Mumbai loss behind to stand any chance of surging ahead in this series. Tendulkar, already under fire, needs to show the world why he is the best. Ponting's retirement has already impacted Tendulkar more than the Aussies. Though his days too are numbered, Sachin has the chance to play a couple of his trademark knocks and retire on a high. It is upto him to grab this chance as time is running out. If this happens, rest assured, the rest are sure to rally around him to put up sizeable totals. In Mumbai, Dhoni complained about his spinners' line and length in the post match conference. For India to win in Kolkata, he should talk to them on the pitch.

But for his leadership role, Dhoni himself would probably not find a place in the line-up. Regarding team composition, with some bounce expected and looking into his past record here, Harbhajan should get a nod which looks highly unlikely. Zaheer is clearly ageing and unless Dhoni picks Ashok Dinda, the local lad, to assist him, the Kolkata Test may expose India's inability to run through English batting yet again.

England are expected to bring Steven Finn in place of Stuart Broad and Ian Bell at the cost of Jonny Bairstow respectively. Why do they want to disturb a winning combination? Their last win here was in 1977. There have been only two English centuries here (Colin Cowdrey, 1964 and Tony Greig, 1977) and their only five wicket haul here came from Bob Willis in 1977. Only second behind Vernon Philander in number of wickets for the year, Broad will be really unlucky if he misses out.

The pitch will be expected to have pace and bounce, contrary to Dhoni's specifications. But one encouraging aspect is, it will be a worn out pitch, which means it will spin. But to exploit the weak English batting, the spin on offer should be of high quality. This is what will test the Indian spinners. Will they deliver? It is meaningless to play three spinners as what two could not do, three could never do.

England have nothing to lose. The onus is on India to deliver and retain their home supremacy which is at stake for the first time. Another slip in Kolkata will see India slide down further. For Dhoni, just standing behind the wickets is not enough. He should lead from the front. With the Australia – South Africa series over, this Test is set to keep everyone on their toes.

At home, India were never on the mat prior to this. For Matt Prior and his mates, this is the best chance!

CHAPTER TEN

HAPLESS INDIA GET MAULED AT HOME

(Week ending December 22, 2012)

After the overseas drubbing and humiliation of 0-4, once each by England and Australia respectively, one expected the Indian team management to go in for drastic changes in the team as well as their attitude. But it looks like the returns for the BCCI as well as the players from the shortest format of the game have blindfolded the authorities and converted them into mute spectators. The series loss to England as a result of the drawn Nagpur Test is the only home series loss in the last one decade by India. This team lead by a clueless M.S. Dhoni has given away the home pride on a platter to the well deserving England team lead from the front by Alastair Cook who has rightly been declared the man of the series.

England's priorities right from the beginning of the tour were to stay focused, practice hard and address the issue of tackling the demon called spin. It is true that there is no substitute for hardwork and England proved this, especially after the recent embarrassment in the gulf in the hands of Pakistan and the lone traumatic defeat in the Ahmedabad Test. This 2-1 comeback win in the Indian sub-continent against a team boasting of stalwarts who are known to be tigers in home conditions, as proved often in the last decade or two, is truly amazing and reaffirms the quality and fighting spirit of this English team. Both the teams lost their no.1 status not long ago. India neither showed any semblance of a fight nor the urge to play like a champion side since then. As a result, they are still tottering in the lower half of the ranking table.

On the other hand, England's pride seems dented by the loss of the crown to South Africa. They came to India with a new skipper, a faction ridden team, their comeback man Kevin Pietersen unsure if he is welcome or not and the not so good reputation of surviving against top class spin. What unfolded subsequently was a script rewritten in style. Barring the first Test where wickets fell like nine pins sans that of Alastair Cook, the team came out shining, with each and every player contributing in his own mighty way. Be it their batsmen, their spin duo or pacer Jimmy Anderson, each one of them played their respective role to telling effect and timed it to perfection. Whenever it mattered, they all stood up. Out of 55 Indian wickets to have fallen during the series, their spinners grabbed 39 and most of the remaining were picked by Anderson.

Indian spinners were supposed to torment the English batsmen. But Panesar and Swann spun a web around the Indian batsmen sans footwork. The Indian bowlers, whose role was to run through their opponents, struggled throughout to even break match winning partnerships. For England, their temperament, commitment, supreme confidence and a cool headed approach ensured they wrap up the series without any hiccups. But for India, the story was totally different.

India had the toss advantage in the first three Tests, got pitches of their choice, played an extra spinner or two in almost all matches and lined up seven batsmen in each Test. All this had no positive impact on a team which did not believe in systematic preparation for the series and were over-confident as well as complacent to the core. They found themselves being lead by a defensive skipper who never thought it necessary to be innovative on the field and seemed to have run out of or was lacking strategies, with no plan B. His own poor form did not help the team's cause either. Their batsmen excelled only in patches and let the team down in critical junctures. This hurt the team's chances and with each failure, the pressure built up on them and made them look not more than a club team playing in a hurry before rushing to the late afternoon movie.

As if these were not enough, the team was riddled with off-field controversies. Criticism of their batting maestro Sachin Tendulkar increased with each failure and calls for the captain's head grew with each defeat. The selectors, always rigid and adamant, failed to take tough calls and only made changes for the final Test which clearly turned out an eye wash. Once world beaters, this team has now lost 10 out of their last 17 Tests. Exactly a year ago, experts were debating whether M.S. Dhoni is turning out to be an all time great Indian captain. He himself has now set to rest all such speculations, thanks to his passive, idea less and dull captaincy. His arrogance and lack of form will probably now place him in the bottom half of Indian captains, similar to the fate his team has suffered in his hands. This home ingnonimity may very soon see a new Test skipper and a different team combination for Team India.

People say form is temporary and class is permanent. After England's most deserving and historic series win, it appears India were only in good form sometime back whereas England were always a class apart!

CHAPTER ELEVEN

INDIAN SPINNERS TURN THE TABLES

(Week ending March 09, 2013)

The Australian batting fragility has been repeatedly exposed on this particular tour of India. Starting from the warm up matches and at the end of the second Test, the visitors, it seems, are under a spell, unable to tackle the Indian spinners. The current imbroglio was much expected as the initial matches in this tour saw Indian Test aspirants walking away with career best figures against this brittle batting line-up. Right from the moment this team was selected, the Australian selection fiasco was thoroughly evident and the selectors' inability to find replacements for Test veterans Ricky Ponting and Mike Hussey gave early indications of the quagmire awaiting them.

Only skipper Michael Clarke has so far carried his fine form forward and it looks like he too is now running out of steam, mainly due to his worries totally not related to his own batting. His boys around him have repeatedly collapsed against the guile of Indian spin on wickets doctored to suit the hosts' spinners. Though the pacemen for India, barring Bhuvaneshwar Kumar in the second Test, did not have any role to play, spinners like Ashwin and part-timer Ravindra Jadeja have become a thorn in the flesh for the Aussie batsmen. Having looked like a rudderless boat against England, Ashwin is oozing with confidence all of a sudden. Jadeja has now almost become the perfect Test all-rounder Dhoni has been looking for though his batting so far has nothing to boast about.

The Australian batting is lined up with players who do not seem to have a fraction of patience and temperament needed to bat in Tests, especially on viciously turning Indian tracks. Also, playing across has brought about most of the Australian downfall so far. Phil Hughes, from whom much was expected, has only 25 runs from four innings. A team with only two batsmen in Clarke and Henriques who had a dream debut, can probably prolong a bit but can never avoid the inevitable rout. Shane Watson, having declared his team's aggressive intention before the series began, looks a shadow of himself and has managed just 77 runs in his four innings. His last Test ton came 37 innings ago.

It is now clear that Clarke needs to move up the batting order and probably play Usman Khawaja and Steven Smith in the upcoming Tests in an attempt to revive their dwindling fortunes. Having scored 4 double tons in 2012 and a century and 91 so far in this series, Clarke is paying for the sins of his batsmen. The press and fans down under are baffled by the spineless display of their team so far. With the Ashes series only a few weeks away, they must be dreading what is in store for them. Clarke's challenge is not his own batting anymore but the combination he picks for the remaining Tests. Will he get it right? Clarke probably has never felt this lonely.

Barring Pattinson in the first Test, the Aussie bowlers too have had a miserable run. Axing Lyon and picking Maxwell for the second Test hasn't gone well with many. For India, this series has been a fairytale so far. Dhoni's fortunes as a skipper and more as a batsman are smiling on him and his ladyluck has come back to him. The Indian batting line-up looks confidence personified. With Tendulkar missing a ton in the first Test, batsmen like Murali Vijay, Cheteshwar Pujara, Kohli and Dhoni too have made hay while the sun shines. Though it is a sorry story for Sehwag till now, a big knock from him too is around the corner, probably in Mohali itself. Though Harbhajan Singh has been bowling well, he must be ruing his inability to take wickets while the rest around him are unable to keep count of their wickets haul. But with the team winning, he is likely to get an extended stint, atleast for now.

While Dhoni became the Indian captain with most Test wins, Clarke has become the first skipper in the world to lose by an innings after declaring the first innings batting first in Hyderabad. As things stand, it looks like a 4-0 sweep to India taking them to the 3rd position in the ICC Test ranking. But knowing how funny this game is, Clarke and his men still have an outside chance to atone for the first couple of lapses. Almost a year ago, India was at the receiving end. It now looks like payback time. Time for regaining the Border-Gavaskar Trophy!

CHAPTER TWELVE

IT'S STEAM INDIA DOWN UNDER

(Week ending January 16, 2021)

Many a Team India fan must surely be worried with the long list of injured players in the current Indian squad touring Australia. This is probably the biggest injured contingent, even bigger than the contingent that was battered in the West Indies in 1976 when India had to lose a match it never contested in spirit. The situation today is such that the Indian team is likely to have only 11 fit players on the day of the Brisbane Test or may be, have the privilege of a readily available 12th man. These injuries sustained are not an indication of cowardice for sure as the guys stood there, braved the repeated bodyline attack and showed why Test cricket is undoubtedly special. The by now famous Sydney draw has overshadowed the biggest injury blow Team India has ever received, the Adelaide Test fiasco where they were looking totally lost and clueless, succumbing with a shameful 36 for 9 to the not so deadly pace attack. Surely, that day left more scars and bruises, in fact countless, on the image of Team India and reaffirmed their perennial dire straits overseas.

From what looked like a certain winning position, India slid to defeat in just under a couple of hours in Adelaide. Was it over confidence? Was it lethargy? God only knows! Test cricket is played session to session and Sourav Ganguly knows this well. It only took a brief power nap for Team India to script a shameful history. So shameful that even the by now infamous 42 all out at Lord's in 1974 will seem ok. It is a known fact that India, especially, in the recent years has been taking lots of pride from it's batting strength. Sheer strength or past records are of no use when a team fails to stand up to it's fans and it's own expectations, that too when at a clear advantage in a crucial series opener. They say the first impression is the best impression and this is what hurt India most in the first Test. When your openers look clueless and give the upper hand to the opponent bowlers in a hurry, the rest are exposed and look clueless too. As if added to these woes, both the rock solid senior batsmen Pujara and Kohli led from the front in India's self-inflicted debacle in Adelaide.

When a team is too proud of it's batting strength, but blind to the same batsmen's miserable overseas history, this was bound to happen sooner than later and it chose Adelaide finally. And in all this self-praise of our batting, the key take away, our bowling, was clearly sidelined and ignored in the recent years. Many of us will remember that there were more instances of declarations by the opposite teams than getting all out against India earlier. It is a matter of pride that Team India's bowling strength, especially the pace attack has been the best ever in the recent years. Our bowlers have repeatedly skittled the opponents twice in a Test, which looked like a rare feat only till recently. Probably, the second innings declaration by the Aussies in Sydney this week came after a long time against India. It was the batsmen who led down the team mostly in the last few years after repeated successful outings by the bowlers. Great teams are made only when the batsmen and bowlers complement each other consistently. The Windies of the 70's and the Aussies of the 90's are two such clear examples. They were undoubtedly the teams that the opponents dreaded to play against.

If Adelaide was a disaster, Melbourne turned out to be the turning point in this series. The team discovered it's lost form and confidence and found it's bearings in the absence of their skipper Kohli. Probably, his return to India has woken them up from their slumber and rekindled their commitment in addition to taking them off lots of peer pressure. They now knew they have come here not only with a mission, but with lots of reputation. The Border-Gavaskar trophy is no less important than the Ashes for the Aussies and for the Indians, it's an opportunity to show the cricketing world why they are deemed the best. Thanks to the injury woes, halfway through the Sydney Test, this team is left with mostly the juniors and debutants, those who want to make a mark in international cricket and transform their respective careers. Till the Sydney Test's 4th innings, almost all players have been in the news either for the injuries or for the lack of form, barring the Melbourne ton by skipper Rahane or the successful entry into international cricket by Shubman Gill. Yes, the late entry of Rohit Sharma has proved a big boost to our batting, though an added hour's stay by him or the Sydney hero Pant would have ensured an Indian win. The whole world is in awe by the way India drew the match, especially in the given circumstances and having to play the last innings of a match staring at a target of over 400 and required to play for almost one and half days.

However, for me, India drew a match which they should have clearly won, again after the lovely opening partnership followed by Pujara's solid stay and Pant's heroics. Pant's rush of blood denied India the victory. However, the Sydney test will be remembered not only for the healing from the bruised reputation but also for the team's standing up to the racial onslaught and emerging successful amidst all this drama and trauma.

It's now time to put all these behind. Going into the Brisbane Test, the woes of Team India are a) KL Rahul and Mayank Aggarwal injured in the nets b) Injuries to pacers Bumrah, Shami and Umesh Yadav c) The only genuine all-rounder Sir Jadeja out of the series d) Vihari, most likely to miss and Ashwin unlikely to play the 4th Test e) Pant still carrying on with the elbow hit and f) Virat Kohli opting out. But the positive is that this team has players hungry to perform, keen to preserve their pride and those with fire in their belly. We now have a majority of youngsters, barring Rohit, Pujara and Rahane probably playing the match, vying for the honours to protect Team India's pride. They are players who have come up in leaps and bounds, seizing every opportunity and capitalizing. They are aware they are yet to be tested but are ready to test their opponents.

It looks like the list of unavailable players now is longer than those available. When your pride is at stake and everything is for the team's sake, nothing else matters. It will be interesting to see the yorker specialist Natarajan make a grand entry and he is surely going to be the trump card for Team India in the bowling section, ably guided by the two S's, super stars Siraj and Saini. Hopefully, one of the senior trio will stand up and make it count. The rest will be inspired not only to follow, but to outdo them as well. The likely composition of the team unlike in the earlier years is no longer a worry for this team. The Sydney Test has turned around the fortunes of this team down under. Not only is the bench strength strong but even those who have been benched are now feeling strong and are hungry and raring to go.

Go India go...! Let the team's steam out...!

CHAPTER THIRTEEN

THIS COOK HAS IMMENSE APPETITE

(Week ending December 08, 2012)

Almost everyone knows December 25 is Christmas day. But exactly 28 years ago, on this day, was born a cricketer who was destined to become England's shining star who has already cooked 23 classic centuries to become England's highest century getter. He is none other than England's skipper Alastair Cook. If consistency has another meaning, it has to be Alastair Cook. It seems this man will never get tired of scoring hundreds.

Having made his Test debut in India in 2006, neither Cook nor his batting style have changed over the years. The promises made by him vide his debut are still being delivered and it looks like this will go on for another couple of decades. He is just nearing 28 and his records are nothing short of amazing, especially those he accomplished in the current tour. Standing 6' 2" and with an ice cool approach, his batting weaves around his own comfort zone. No rush of blood and no unforced errors. He knows how to stay there, unperturbed and by doing so, he is aware runs will not only follow, but flow.

Though he has been made the skipper only recently, he has led England from the front in recent times. He has been there, busy piling runs, whenever his team needed them. Most deservingly, he is the youngest to reach 7,000 Test runs. He has captained England 5 times till date and he has 5 hundreds to his credit as captain. In the process, he has scored most runs as an English skipper, leaving behind Ted Dexter. He could not have asked for a better moment than scoring his 23rd hundred in Kolkata in Ted Dexter's presence.

If we take the current series alone, he already has 3 Test centuries preceded by 119 and 97 respectively in two warm-up games. He has now faced most deliveries in a series in the sub-continent for England, more than Dennis Amiss' 1176. If he continues to play like this in the remaining innings of this series, he is set to surpass Ken Barrington and Mike Gatting for the highest series aggregate in the sub-continent by an Englishman.

He isn't an aggressive batsman, but a silent killer. No wonder he has only hit 9 sixers in his 151 innings so far. The pitches on offer and the bowlers at India's disposal had no impact on Cook's batting. Inspite of turning tracks and lethal Indian spin options, it is Cook who has stood between the two sides, giving ample confidence to his fellow batsmen and helping them overcome the first Test fiasco. The Indians must have been ruing the two let offs Cook received on his way to 190 before getting comically run out. But probably they aren't aware this is only a breather before the final Test begins shortly.

Michael Clarke might have scored 4 double tons in 2012 and Hashim Amla might have been scoring in every alternate innings, but Cook's display is consistency personified and he has been the most prolific run getter in international cricket. With his self-belief and immense concentration, he has seldom returned to the pavilion with the task on hand left unfinished. If England managed to win The Ashes in Australia after 24 years, it is purely because of this man who managed an incredible aggregate of 766 runs in 7 innings. In the process, he became the second youngest after Sachin Tendulkar to reach 5,000 Test runs. His aggregate for 2012 as on date is a magical 1,234 and it is unfortunate he hasn't been able to score a double in this year yet.

Not only for Australia in the recent times and for India now, he is set to remain a nemesis for many a team in the coming years. In the modern era of limited overs cricket, if there are very few orthodox and traditional cricketers who relish, excel in and continue bringing us cricket in it's classic form, Cook leads that pack without any doubt. As Sunil Gavaskar rightly pointed out, he is destined to reach 15,000 runs and 50 centuries with ease and it is only a matter of time before he does it as he thoroughly deserves it!

Inspite of Andrew Strauss' recent retirement, Pietersen's on and off appearance and most of the other batsmen's lack of form, Cook has been rallying the team around him, thanks to his commitment, consistency and hunger to perform!

CHAPTER FOURTEEN

BCCI WILL CONTINUE TO FLEX IT'S FINANCIAL MUSCLE
(Week ending March 26, 2014)

The Board Of Control For Cricket In India(BCCI) is coming under increasing attack – from within and outside the country. First, it was Tony Greig and then, it was Arjuna Ranatunga. It did not end there. An overwhelming 69% of the international cricketers surveyed recently opined that the BCCI influences International Cricket Council's(ICC) decision making. In effect, the image of the apex body for cricket worldwide has taken a severe dent.

The IPL is being seen as a money-making monster that is luring players to the detriment of national interest. The subtle pressure that was brought upon by the BCCI ensured that Sri Lanka had to relent in allowing some of their key players stay in India to prolong their stay in the IPL while the national team was preparing for the tour of England. In fact, the lucrative Indian Premier League(IPL) is perceived as the reason for Lasith Malinga bidding adieu to international cricket – a huge loss for Sri Lanka.

That the BCCI is a cash-rich entity is beyond any shadow of doubt. That it does not hesitate to flex its financial muscle to get its way with the ICC is what is causing a lot of heartburn around the world.

The season four of IPL, which followed even before the Indian team players could soak in the joy of winning the World Cup, put enormous stress and strain on the players who were in the thick of World Cup action. Not surprisingly, the casualty list kept increasing by the day... Virender Sehwag, Gautam Gambhir and Yuvraj Singh to add to the nonavailability of captain Mahendra Singh Dhoni, Sachin Tendulkar and Zaheer Khan. That's almost half the side that did duty for India!

Even as the Country versus Club debate rages on, the public perception is that the BCCI is more interested in raking the moolah than caring for the country or the players.

The tour of the Caribbean offers a great chance for India to close in on Australiain the ICC ODIrankings as well as reiterate their supremacy as the No.1 ranked Test playing nation, but in the absence of several key players, the task will be that much more onerous.

A proactive board with a heightened sense of national interest would have done all within its means to ensure that Sehwag and Gambhir did not aggravate their injuries by ensuring that they got adequate rest before the Caribbean tour. It would have done all within its means to do the same for Dhoni and Tendulkar so that they were fresh and available for the West Indies tour. But the intent was never evident and neither there was any sense of remorse.

The unpleasant impact of the IPL is already evident with many international cricketers retiring early to ensure they rake in more money in shorter time by remaining fresh and fit for the IPL.

But would the criticism change things or rattle the BCCI? No way! As the saying goes, “He who has the gold, makes the rules.” Like it or lump it.

CHAPTER FIFTEEN

IMPORTANCE OF MULTI-TASKING DHONI TO INDIA

Not since the days of Kapil Dev has an Indian who is not a frontline batsman created a major impact with his batting as Mahendra Singh Dhoni.

Ever since his debut –ODI's in 2004 and Test in 2005 – Dhoni's savagely unorthodox batting has made his stock in international cricket soar like mercury on a scorching summer afternoon. His Tests & ODIs combined pool of 11 hundreds and 57 fifties speaks volumes for his credentials in front of the wicket. That he has the added burden of captaincy and the demanding job of a keeper makes his success all the more spectacular.

He is not just another player who got the position of leading the side merely on the basis of seniority. He earned his captaincy on merit at a young age and has played a significant role in India attaining pole position in international cricket. He has marshaled his resources to help India win the inaugural T20 World Cup and as captain of India in Tests, has not lost a single series.

Dhoni was under two years old when Kapil Dev's Indian team won the 1983 World Cupin England. Since then, the Indian team has never looked so good to win the World Cup yet as it is now in the 2011 edition. And in Dhoni, India has one of the coolest leaders in the history of cricket with a proven track record as captain.

Dhoni leads by example. In the warm-up game againstNew Zealand, he roared back into form with a timely century – a knock that will do both him and the Indian team immense good. An off-form captain – especially in a major event like the World Cup – does not augur well for the team and Dhoni's recent hundred would have made the Indian team quite buoyant.

It's not easy for bowlers to bowl to Dhoni or for captains to set field for a batsman who is unconventional in the extreme. His brutal attacks have changed the course of a game in a jiffy and that is something oppositions would be most mindful of a batsman coming lower down.

Despite its awesome reputation, the Indian batting line-up has not lived up to it's expectations in recent times. In fact, it's the bowlers who have played a major role in most of our recent victories.

As a team best equipped to winning the world cup, India needs Dhoni the batsman as much as it needs Dhoni the captain.

CHAPTER SIXTEEN

IRELAND REKINDLE INDIA'S NATWEST TROPHY HEROICS (Week ending March 02, 2011)

Ireland handed a stunning defeat to England and in the process, taught quite a few lessons to the formidableworld cup teams. In what was a replay of the famous Natwest Trophy final between India and England, Ireland made mincemeat of the English attack with the only difference being, the Irish skipper did not remove his shirt this time around and Andrew Flintoff wasn't present on the ground. India need to take a leaf out of Ireland's book if they nurture hopes of progressing beyond the quarterfinal stage of this world cup.

Just like India who were reeling with five wickets down for 146 against England in the 2002 Natwest series final, Ireland was pinned to the wall at 111 for five. This was a stage when everyone in the ground would have drawn the inevitable conclusion and mentally awarded victory to England with a resolution to leave the ground. Except, may be, the English coach Andy Flower who had no choice but to believe that everything was over. Just to compare the two famous matches involving England, if India were chasing 326, Ireland were chasing 327. If India lost five wickets before Yuvraj Singh and Mohammad Kaif scripted a sensational turnaround, Ireland lost their five wickets a wee bit earlier.

Ireland's stunning fightback was masterminded by Kevin O'Brien and Cusack, who staged an unparalleled show never seen before in the world cup history. In the process, O'Brein reached his 100 off just 50 deliveries, eclipsing the world cup record of the fastest hundred (in 66 balls) by Matthew Hayden. O'Brien's innings was an epic as big as Kapil Dev's 175 not out when with India reeling at 17 for five. For the simple reason that O'Brien's innings of 113 off 63 deliveries was for a cause chasing an improbable uphill task of chasing 328.

England got away with a win in the first match against a deserving Netherlands and with a tie subsequently. But Ireland completed the unfinished task of Netherlands by turning the tables on England. If ICC has announced their intentions to keep away the minnows from the next edition of the world cup, Ireland gave a fitting reply to the apex body. Ireland's performance against England is a wake-up call for the established teams.

Ireland ensured that the match will certainly go down as one of the biggest, best and thrilling chases in the history of the cricket world cup. If the India-England tie brought this world cup alive, the Irish chase was an icing on the cake.

CHAPTER SEVENTEEN

IT'S A TOSS-UP BETWEEN KOHLI AND RAINA (World Cup 2011)

Team India for the world cup is undoubtedly the strongest on paper, looking into the recent and immediate past individual batting performances. Such is the embarrassment of batting riches that talented and deserving batsmen often necessarily have to sit out.

What the team needs is stability in the middle overs for the men with the firepower later to launch the final assault. The one slot in the middle order for which Suresh Raina and Virat Kohli will be vying for will be critical to India's batting fortunes in this world cup.

Sachin Tendulkar, Virender Sehwag, Gautam Gambhir and Yusuf Pathan are certainties in the final eleven. Yuvraj Singh, a proven match winner, but the most consistently inconsistent batsman of late, is also likely to be seen in action in the first few matches to cement his place.

His current form does not make him an automatic choice in the eleven, but his track record and proven all-round abilities warrant he gets preferential treatment in the initial stages.

The absence of a left-arm spinner in the squad enhances Yuvraj's selection claims as skipperMahendra Singh Dhoni could well do with that variety and option in the bowling resources at his command. Yuvraj has, more than once, risen to the occasion at critical times in vital matches for India – Stuart Broad will vouch for that!

This leaves two young hearts in Raina and Kohli battling to fill in the remaining batting slot. Both deserve it in their own right. While Raina holds the edge as a senior pro and a tested batsman, Kohli's form and knack of grabbing opportunities with both hands will be given serious consideration by the selectors.

Raina's early promise was dented for a while in the Greg Chapell era. He lost his confidence when he was made to bat in almost all positions. His confidence came back under the leadership of Dhoni for Chennai Super

Kings. While his recent lack of form and temperament will be a setback, his athletic fielding and ability to hit deep over the fence will be plusses in his favour.

On the other hand, Kohli has played a big hand in India's ODI success in the last one year. He was India's best bet and if cricket had an award for the "Best & Promising Youngster", Kohli would have no serious contest to bag the honours. His tenure at the wicket always gives the impression that he is one of the seniors with a specific purpose of not only stabilizing the innings but also dominating the bowling attack with disdain.

Fortunately for Dhoni, despite the handicap of having one batsman less in the squad, he can afford different permutations and combinations in the batting line-up, thanks to these two.

India is one of the most formidable batting outfits not only due to the individual talents, but also due to the various options it has at its command. If Kohli gives an extra 30 runs due to his batting, Raina is sure to cut the opposition total by at least 30 runs through his brilliance on the field. Both are match winners in their own right and will surely cash in on any slip by Yuvraj or Pathan. If Dhoni, too, returns to form, no total will appear small to chase.

Dhoni is a shrewd captain and knows how to play his cards. He also knows Indian middle order is like a piece of shining glass that needs to be handled with care.

CHAPTER EIGHTEEN

MANY IPL4 STARS PREFERRED CLUB OVER COUNTRY

Gone are the days when only Maggie sauce used to be different from the rest. The just-ended IPLedition can proudly claim to have joined that elite list. IPL has always had something or the other to offer. If it was wholesome entertainment to the innumerable cricket fans, it was also an opportunity to stake a claim on an international cricketing career, accompanied by fame and money. In addition to these, each season of IPL always offered something to ponder about. This has been one of the rare cricketing events where we have seen the venue shifted from one country to another, the organizing chairman sacked and with which the Bollywood, though indirectly, and cheerleaders are associated with.

This IPL saw the retiring Shane Warne warned before being fined US $50,000 for his tirade against the Rajasthan Cricket Association secretary. This should be one of the rarest farewells as well. Instead of receiving a farewell gift, Warne had to shell out this huge amount through his nose. What a send-off for a legend who led a bunch of no-hopers to victory in the first edition of the IPL!

This IPL has seen many of the world cup winning Indian players sidelined by injuries and niggles. It's a pity that the cricket-loving West Indies public will not get to see many of the big names that won the 2011 World Cup.

IPL4 triggered the Country vs Club debate, leading to two Indian cricketing legends – Sunil Gavaskar and Kapil Dev – differing in their respective views on the matter.

The West Indies Board seems to have towed Gavaskar's line by sidelining IPL hero Chris Gayle, by ignoring his heroics and abilities, along with Jerome Taylor. This means the world's best T20 batsman will not feature in the T20 match against India. Shame! While Gayle preferred the IPL to his country, the West Indies Cricket Board preferred not to use his services, atleast for the time being.

The 2011 edition of the IPL witnessed quite a few empty seats at the match venues. Surely, the 51-day affair with around 70 matches was a bit too much after the world cup feast. The initial IPL editions saw some international cricketers preferring country to club and thus keeping away from this abridged entertainment. This time saw a turnaround with many a cricketer preferring club to country. Not surprisingly, many of the Orange and Purple cap owners in IPL4 were those who preferred club over country.

IPL, the most lucrative short-term assignment was expected to bring out fresh and young talent, especially with the opportunity it provides to youngsters to mix with national as well as foreign international cricketers. The Indian selectors did not consider even one youngster from this IPL worth touring the West Indies. Just like this shorter version, players thrown into limelight also live in the public memory for a short duration. IPL has hitherto provided a shortcut to get into Team India. But are these youngsters really tested thoroughly? May be one in a few might come up with a whirlwind knock on his day. Anybody claiming a slot in the national team should undergo the test by playing domestic fixtures like Ranjior Duleep Trophy. This will atleast give a semblance of assurance that they can stand the test at international level with their temperament and endurance. Can the IPL achieve this?

As an Indian fan, I would prefer an IPL which makes a difference and not one which is just different.

CHAPTER NINETEEN

MARK BOUCHER LEAVES HIS MARK

(Week ending July 14, 2012)

It is very unfortunate, South Africa had to bid farewell to their star keeper-cum-batsman Mark Boucher under unforeseen circumstances. Boucher had indeed made a mark for himself in international cricket. He has most dismissals behind the wickets, holds the record for the second highest run-getter wicket keeper behind Adam Gilchrist of Australia and has played the highest no. of Tests as a wicket keeper. Though he was already contemplating retirement after the end of the all important tour against England, this injury to his left eye was in store for him. Boucher, hit by a flying bail has returned home and A B De Villiers has been named as his replacement behind the stumps.

His premature retirement and exit from the forthcoming tour has left his teammates shell shocked, but each one of them will do his best to beat England and wrest the no.1 rank from the hosts, atleast for Boucher's sake. His statistics as a keeper leave his peers way behind. The third Test at Lords would have made him the first keeper to have played 150 Tests, another 2 dismissals would have made him the first keeper to effect 1,000 dismissals and another meagre 56 runs would have seen him as the keeper to have scored highest number of runs in Tests. But fate was cruel to him and the game as it had different ideas which saw the records which were within reach remain a dream now and his dreams shattered. His 555 Test dismissals place him way ahead of everyone else whilst his 424 ODI dismissals leave him 48 behind Adam Gilchrist. It was indeed special watching him in international action for 14 years.

On the other side, England will take pride from their landmark performance against the Aussies in the just concluded ODI series. Rain played spoil sport to limit their win in the 5 match series to 4-0. This defeat is the worst suffered by the Kangaroos in 40 years and is a perfect reflection of England's current consistent form and dominance in international cricket. No wonder for England, the win in the last ODI was their 10th ODI win in succession. This series result will leave one wondering whether this is the same Aussies of the yesteryears. In their last 29 ODI's, they have won 13, lost 14, tied 1 and one match saw no result, unlike their usual confident and dominant self.

Back in the Caribbean, the Kiwis came back strongly to hand the West Indies a 88 run defeat in the 3rd ODI, to make it 1-2, thereby inducing some interest in the series with two matches remaining. While the hosts still remain the favourites, they will be aware they cannot afford to take the Kiwis lightly as they can bounce back anytime from nowhere.

The 209 run win in the first Test at Galle for Sri Lanka ensured the Lankans just needed to play smart cricket in the remaining two Tests to ensure they walk away with a 1-0 series win. Both these drawn Tests were hampered by rain, an usual phenomenon in Sri Lanka at this time of the year. It was a pity, Pakistan's efforts in creating winning situations were thwarted jointly by the Lankans and the weather Gods alike.

CHAPTER TWENTY

CHAMPIONS OF A DIFFERENT LEAGUE

(Week ending October 20, 2012)

It is an open secret that the ongoing Champions League T20 is skewed towards IPL teams. It clearly is not in line with it's philosophy of holding a T20 championship between the club teams of various ICC member countries. With 10 teams forming part of the main draw, it is surprising to see a complete imbalance as far as representation from various countries is concerned. There is no dispute that this is a very lucrative league and looking into the current trend amongst international cricketers, most of the teams would die to come and play here.

Four Indian teams, two each from Australia and South Africa and one each from England and New Zealand taking part is nothing but complete mockery of the intended composition. It does not mean India can walk away with a large piece of the cake just because BCCI is the brainchild behind this whole concept. Teams from other countries who have fared as well as or are equal to the IPL teams' standards have to undergo the gruelling qualifiers only to be eliminated at a later stage as there are only two available slots. It is beyond imagination as to how many budding cricketers' prospects of a golden international career are nipped in the bud when their respective teams failed to make the cut.

When the IPL teams play at home, there is no match to them and every player is a hero and every team is a potential champion. But from the day the champions league began, these teams' vulnerability to sportive pitches has been thoroughly exposed. Only Delhi Daredevils have won a match till date, that too against their local rivals Kolkata Knight Riders. Failing to register a win in their first three matches, Kolkata, the recent IPL champions, are the first team to bow out with disgrace. Chennai Super Kings who had won former IPL and CL editions with ease seem to have lost their midas touch to lose their first two matches and are on the verge of following Kolkata's footsteps. It was a pity to see the reigning champions Mumbai Indians and

Chennai Super Kings being tamed and mauled by Highveld Lions who came into the competition as clear underdogs.

Though most of the teams are a mixture of international stars, the non-IPL teams have done reasonably well so far and they were quick and the first to adapt to the unique South African conditions. The sub-continent teams are still grappling with the alien conditions and are clueless against the bounce and pace on offer on these wickets. Ten innings so far from the Indian batsmen have produced just one fifty. A closer diagnosis will reveal pathetic performances by each one of them. The remaining matches will surely be an acid test for these teams as they are now entering a must win phase.

BCCI has once again allowed their stars to play the shorter format with a no. of Tests matches due in the next few days. The BCCI has neither learnt from it's mistakes nor taken a leaf out of Cricket Australia who pulled out Shane Watson from CLT20 halfway to enable him focus on the forthcoming Tests against the Proteas.

The IPL teams are surely struggling and seem to be champions of a different league!

CHAPTER TWENTY-ONE

CLASH OF THE TITANS BEGINS

(Week ending July 21, 2012)

The much awaited Test series between England and South Africa has begun. This series will be a litmus test for the hosts as well as the Proteas and will see a titanic clash for Test supremacy. The tour will be a long and grinding one as these rivals are set to play 3 Tests, 5 ODI's and 3 T20's. The Test series is a must win for both as a win for the Proteas will propel them to the top spot and a win or draw for England will ensure they continue their stay at the helm.

Though the first Test of the close contests is already underway, it will be foolish to pick a favourite and wise to wait till the end for the results. The toss favoured England and inspite of losing their skipper in the first over, the hosts recovered through an excellent partnership of 170. Having allowed England to reach a sizeable total, it will be an uphill task for the Proteas to wrest control of this Test.

Team India will be back on the field later today to play international cricket after a long gap. Though the players are fresh and raring to go, they would prefer to forget and put behind the last 12 months following their world cup win. It has been one of the worst periods of Indian cricket when the team lost 8 overseas Tests in a row, failed to qualify for the Tri-series finals in Australia as well as the Asia Cup finals in Bangladesh inspite of being the world cup holders. They will be seen in action in Sri Lanka playing 5 ODI's and a lone T20.

Coming to team selections, Kevin Pietersen's bid to make a comeback to help England retain the T20 world cup was thwarted when the selectors did not name him in the provisional list. This has nothing to do with his class or form but relates to issues outside the field. This selection snub may see the end of Kevin's T20 career. For India, Yuvraj Singh, the hero of the world cup triumph is back in action. Two key inclusions in the T20 world cup probables for India are Yuvraj and Harbhajan Singh. Whilst Yuvraj is successfully back after battling cancer, Harbhajan was picked inspite of battling his poor form. It will be great if these two make it to the final fifteen but it looks an uphill task for Harbhajan.

In a surprise move, South Africa included Graeme Smith and Jacques Kallis in the T20 world cup probables list. The last time Smith and Kallis represented their nation in T20 was in this February and mid 2010 respectively.

For the West Indies, it was a well deserved 4-1 ODI series victory against New Zealand at home. Though the last match was only of academic interest, the hosts were determined to wrap up yet another win. Though their top order failed yet again, the lower order rose to the occasion with vital contributions for the second time in succession to rescue their team. In addition to this, the Kiwis who have been clueless against and were tormented throughout by the mystery spinner Sunil Narine, finally gave him his first well deserved five wicket haul in the last match.

CHAPTER TWENTY-TWO

CONSISTENCY, THE SUCCESS MANTRA

(Week ending April 28, 2012)

Much was expected from Ricky Ponting when the Kangaroos began their Test series against the West Indies. This was the specific reason inspite of being dropped from the ODI squad, he was retained for the longer version. However, this tour turned out a disappointment not only for the selectors, but for Ponting himself as well. With a highest score of 57 in three Tests, Ponting looked a totally different batsman from the one who played against the Indians recently at home. Amidst this failure, he became the second highest run getter in Test cricket after Sachin Tendulkar when he overtook Rahul Dravid. This is certainly no mean achievement and is a testament to Ricky's tested abilities and gigantic achievements during the last two decades. Ponting's batting heroics over the years have certainly taken the Aussie dominance over the rest of the world to an unparalleled level in the past.

The hosts' inability to wrap up the second half of the Aussie innings continued into the third Test. It was Wade's turn this time to script a turnaround after most of the top order batsmen succumbed to the Windies' attack in the first innings. He hit a stylish ton with the support of the tailenders to take the Aussies past the 300 mark. This was followed by the typical collapse yet again by the Caribbeans, notwithstanding the heroics of Chanderpaul yet again which gave their total some respectability. Though the Windies came back well to skittle the visitors for less than 300 in their second outing, the target of 370 began with early hiccups with the Windies losing 3 quick wickets. With a day to spare, it looks like it will be difficult for the West Indies to survive the Aussie onslaught on this deteriorating wicket. Any chances of Sammy's team reaching the target looks unlikely with the absence of clean hitters like Chris Gayle, Dwayne Bravo and Kieron Pollard who are busy doing their IPL duties. May be, Chanderpaul has different ideas!

It has been a roller-coaster ride for most of the IPL teams. The only team which has managed to remain within the top two positions for more than two weeks continuosly is Delhi Dare Devils. Players like Kevin Pietersen and Jayawardene joining the team after the first few days and Sehwag hitting great form have boosted the team's chances in this edition. It is to be seen how the team management will accommodate David Warner when he joins them after finishing his current national commitments in West Indies. Mumbai Indians, Royal Challengers Bangalore and Chennai Super Kings are struggling to live up to expectations. Inspite of the very mediocre beginning, Chennai and Bangalore were fortunate to recover lost ground by winning their last few matches respectively.

It is quite surprising a competition played in the dawn of the summer in India is affected by rains. Two matches during the week had to be abandoned due to unseasonal storms which hit just before the matches were to begin. This enabled Deccan Chargers, the winner of the second edition of the IPL to earn their first point after losing the initial 5 matches. May be, this boosted their confidence to go on and earn their first win when they beat Pune Warriors. It was a great sight to watch Yuvraj Singh at the ground cheering his team on their home ground Pune. Though the Warriors and the local crowd gave him an emotional welcome as he is just back from his treatment, it was heartening to see his team failing to beat the Deccan Chargers. But seeing Yuvraj on the ground has given clear indications he is well on the road to recovery and it will not be long before his fans can see the live wire back in action.

As on date, it looks like only Delhi Dare Devils are assured of a place in the last four, especially with their current high confidence levels and consistency. The remaining slots can go to any of the three teams from the other teams barring Deccan Chargers. This is because, the Deccans, even if they strike form and find winning ways, may realize they have woken up a bit late and have already missed the bus. None of these teams have so far managed to play consistent cricket to claim a rightful place in the last four. Pune Warriors, led by their astute skipper Sourav Ganguly, initially exceeded all expectations by beating big guns like Delhi, Mumbai and Chennai. Their inability to play consistent cricket saw them remain in the 6th spot after their loss to Deccan Chargers. A win here would have taken them to the second spot in the points table. This is how fortunes have been fluctuating in this IPL. Let's wait and see as the race has just begun!

CHAPTER TWENTY-THREE

CRICKETERS' ENCOUNTERS AND ACHIEVEMENTS

(Week ending April 14, 2012)

After the successful treatment of his malignant tumour, Yuvraj Singh is now expected to return to competitive cricket if not immediately, sometime later this year. With the innumerable matches being played in the shorter format, players like Yuvraj will make a big impact for their respective teams. Inspired by Lance Armstrong who underwent similar trauma in his life and emerged a winner, Yuvraj brushed aside the gloomy side of his predicament to remain positive and qualify for yet another long cricketing innings. The week also saw another great achievement by the former Lankan skipper Kumara Sangakkara when he was chosen as Wisden's leading cricketer of the year as well as one of the 5 Wisden Cricketers of the year for 2011 respectively. This is the first time anyone has achieved this dual distinction since the birth of Wisden's leading cricketer award in 2004. The other 4 Wisden cricketers are England's Alistair Cook and Tim Bresnan alongwith Lancashire captain Glen Chapple and fellow pacer Alan Richardson. Tim Bresnan also has the rare distinction of not figuring on the losing side in a Test match yet.

The first Test between Australia and West Indies went to the wire on expected lines. After scoring more than 400 in the first innings, the Windies had the Kangaroos' back to the wall. Instead of taking a sizeable first innings lead, the hosts managed a slender lead, that too when the rival skipper made a strategic declaration to give his bowlers a chance to skittle the Windies in their second outing to set up an improbable win. This, the Aussie bowlers did in style. However, their batsmen made the target of 192 look uphill only to manage to win the match by 3 wickets. The continued absence of Christ Gayle at the top of the batting order is certainly hitting the West Indies quite hard.

England won their second Test against Sri Lanka to square the series and also retain their no.1 Test ranking. Reaching the top and managing to stay there are qualities of a champion side and England posses this in abundance.

Every time IPL is played, a couple of stars are born and this edition is no exception. Already the current IPL has seen a debutant IPL player, Kevon Cooper leading the wicket takers' table possessing the purple cap in the process. With his consistent all-round performance, he has also won the hearts of one and all. His initial aspiration was to play alteast one game for his team Rajasthan Royals. His first match saw him getting a 4 wicket haul and he began his IPL batting with a first ball six followed by a four. This was his own way of taking the competition by storm. Just a year ago, his bowling action during the Carribean T20 was suspect. Luckily for him, his government sent him to Australia to work on his action. Coming from a family of footballers, Cooper was depressed and lost hopes on a cricketing future. But today, he stands tall in India amongst cricketing greats and is now ready to make a mark in international cricket for his country in the near future, atleast in the shorter version. Though he has already represented his team back home in the champions league, his IPL performance will surely bring him to limelight. No wonder, his team Rajasthan Royals, the IPL champions in the first edition is today looking upto him, the star of this IPL, to deliver them victories.

Already this IPL is turning out to be one of mixed fortunes for teams. Teams expected to walk over their opponents are seen losing matches and underdogs are sitting pretty after a few matches. With each team bound to play 16 league matches in the 45 day tournament, there is bound to be uncertainity till the half-way stage as to which teams will make it to the last four. However, as the second half unfolds, clearer picture will start emerging and it will be possible to distinguish between good teams and also rans. As on date, the best team on paper, Mumbai Indians, are leading the table. With Kevin Pietersen and Mahela Jayawardene joining their team, Delhi Dare Devils convincingly thrashed the holders Chennai Super Kings to closely follow the leaders. The surprise pack so far has been Pune Warriors India led by former India skipper Sourav Ganguly. They won the first two matches in style, only to lose the third to Kings XI Punjab and are placed third. Chennai moved from 7th to 5th position, thanks to their record chase of 205 against Royal Challengers Bangalore, the second best ever chase in IPL history. This is only the beginning and the days ahead will see high scoring games!

Encounters on and off the field bring out the hero in cricketers resulting in supreme achievements.

CHAPTER TWENTY-FOUR

IT'S TIME FOR THE MASTER'S MASTERSTROKE

(Week ending February 23, 2013)

Sachin Tendulkar is set to take on the Aussies probably for the final time in his career when the four Test series at home begins this Friday. Will he be India's man Friday for one last time? Will he retire on a high? The time for him to retire passed by a couple of years ago, after India's world cup triumph. That was the best moment for him to quit after having won his dream world cup which took him almost half a dozen world cups to be fulfilled. But he chose to miss it.

He carried on, trusting his abilities to the fullest. Though he has scored in patches, most of them being contributions in vain, especially during the twin 0-4 drubbing in the hands of England and Australia respectively post world cup and the recent 1-2 mauling his team received from England at home. Every time he failed, he looked up to domestic cricket to regain his touch, which he did. But the script in international cricket remained the same. This resulted in his reluctant retirement from ODI's in December 2012 just before India locked horns with Pakistan, the most favourite opponents for them. Only Tendulkar was absent, but the team's fortunes remained the same, losing the battle 1-2.

Tendulkar is short of 16,000 Test runs just by 355. No one in Test cricket is yet to achieve this milestone and this will soon be yet another feather in his cap. His recent domestic stint gave him two hundreds and more than that, must have given him ample confidence. His recent disasters on the field increased calls for his immediate retirement from one and all. So pathetic were his scores, the manner and mode of dismissals, that his most ardent fans were the first ones to call for his early exit from the Indian cricket scene. Many cricket pundits in India and the world over were of the same view, but chose the diplomatic path in joining the retirement cries and cleverly put the ball in the selector's court. The end of 2012 ended Tendulkar's ODI career inspite of his conveying his availability for the

Pakistan series to the selectors just a day before. Only a few were shocked.

His preference to carry on in the Test scene must be attributed to his immense self-confidence and should never be interpreted as arising out of other considerations. Even today, he undoubtedly looks the best of the Indian batsmen, always raising hopes of yet another hundred in the making. His recent failures were mostly due to his over cautious approach rather than lack of form. A man who has lived international cricket most of his life would certainly like to quit on a high. There cannot be a better occasion than doing it against the mighty and his favourite opponents Australia. The four Tests and probably around 6 to 8 innings are bound to show us the vintage Sachin for one last time and it will not be a surprise if he adds another ton or two before the end of this series.

11 of his 51 Test centuries have come against the Aussies at an astounding average of 60.59 alongwith 13 fifties from just 31 Tests. With 2 double tons against them, he has been the batsman most feared by the Aussies. His last double century was against them in 2010-11 in Bengaluru in a match winning cause. When he entered the international scene in 1989 against Pakistan, the world saw in him a boy with a braveheart. Today, the boy as well as the braveheart are still present in him. His longevity, as appreciated by Michael Clarke, has shown no signs of fatigue or wear and tear. When he takes guard in the first Test on Friday, he will remain as fresh as he always was.

The previous series against the Aussies was the first for Sachin without a century against them. Neither Dravid nor Laxman will be by his side against the Kangaroos now. This will not deter him. He has already proved his class to the world umpteen times. But this time, he will be playing for himself, his pride. A man who waited for two decades to lift the world cup will surely know why he is still around. He must have by now set a few personal milestones before this series ends. Millions have rejoiced his batting. They will be awaiting his bat to wield his magic for one last time. It will for sure and that will be the moment the master will call it a day. Having remained unconquered throughout his career, Tendulkar will never quit a loser, but will go with his head held high.

His last hurrah against the Aussies has no room for submission. He is on a mission!

CHAPTER TWENTY-FIVE

ASHES' SEE-SAW BATTLE IN FULL SWING

(Week ending July 25, 2015)

The five Test Investec Ashes series has begun on expected lines with the two teams sharing honours in the first two Tests. While England decimated the Aussies in the first, it was the Aussies who mauled England in the second. With three Tests remaining, the team which can manage to win the third Test will certainly go into the fourth with its head as well as morale high.

Australia lost the first Test in a manner that will cause them much disquiet. While England was not far from them in the second. Both teams gave in in typical fashion in respective Tests. Having had to chase, they both succumbed without a trace of a fight in a toothless batting display which thoroughly exposed their lack of temperament which is a must, especially when one is chasing big targets on a fourth or fifth day of a Test.

England won the first Test by a margin of 169 runs. Joe Root, man of the match for his decisive first-innings hundred, even chipped in with a couple of wickets and the final catch. The favourites beaten at the first attempt were sure to bounce back in the second and they did it in style. Pundits doubted if England's attack had the capacity to dismiss Australia twice. But they ensured they did the needful with confidence. Almost all of the English players contributed in bits and pieces. While the bowlers were disciplined, Root chipped in with lower order wickets and the catch which sealed their win. It was also surprising to see Nathan Lyon and Moeen Ali coming up with contrasting performances on the same wicket. If Lyon took four wickets on the previous day, Moeen Ali overcame his initial expensive spell to come back with a crucial two wicket haul.

England's performance was more or less clinical and quite satisfying. Inspite of being unlucky initially, their bowlers persisted with line and length, passing the bat quite often. Though the swing available earlier in the match was absent, England pulled back their lengths slightly, hoping that a dry and variable surface would aid them. Finally, they were rewarded with five Australian wickets for 25 in 12 overs which was definitely an emphatic turnaround.

Joe Root was dropped on nought by Haddin in the first Test and he capitalised on it very well. Root's form in the last year or so has been exceptional: 1,513 runs at an average of 79.63 since June 2014.

Like a trapeze artist learning to live without a safety net, England found out at Lord's that Joe Root will not always be able to conceal the cracks in their top order. England had got away sometimes with a poor start as they have a long order with Moeen Ali batting as low as no.8. But lady luck failed to smile on them this time. England never recovered after losing 3 early wickets. They simply did not have any safety net this time around. On recent occasions, England has lost their first 3 wickets within 50, a state very undesirable for a team hoping to put up a large total. England's opening pair had been very fragile in the recent past and no team can afford it. Poor Lyth has been a consistent failure, always struggling to handle quality pace bowling whilst skipper Alistair Cook is busy trying to regain his midas touch.

An apparent air of resignation hung around Lord's as England bowled for five sessions whereas the Aussies seemed urgent and desperate when they bowled. Perhaps it was superior skill, and superior confidence in them. Whilst England looked rattled and hurried in their batting, the Kangaroos remained cool and kept their calm throughout. The visitors were smart enough to go hard at the hosts, never giving them any breathing space. Once Lyth went, the Aussies smelt blood while England looked lost and rattled. It is only five Test innings since Lyth made a century against a strong New Zealand attack and this tiny record will leave England in a dilemma whether to axe him or play him for the rest of the series.

This is exactly the time when England's senior players, their batsmen in particular need to deliver in the rest of the series. We have seen what happens to them once Cook and/or Root fail. Another notable concern for England is the consistent failure of their ever reliable Ian Bell and the alarm bells are certainly being heard ringing aloud now.

Bell looked perplexed when he was bowled. It will be better for Bell and England if he starts playing straight and in the V for the remainder of the series as the gaps between his bat and pad and in his batting in general are becoming wider by the day. Bell has the best technique in the English side. He will now agree that the new ball is better played straight than with an angled bat. The pressure on him is growing for sure. One good thing England have done for the third Test is to bring in Bairstow for Gary Ballance. Hope this restores some Balance in their brittle batting. England should consider promoting Root to No. 3.

Now that both teams are level, it is the team that holds its nerves will prevail in the remainder of the series. Teams should take it session by session. A small lapse in one session may cost the series. Knowing fully well the Aussies are hungrier once they smell blood, England will have their task cut out. Their bowlers are bowling well in tandem, but they need the support of their batsmen. Especially, a strong start and a huge first inning lead only can come to England's aid.

Australia do not win Ashes regularly on English soil. But surely, this is one of their best chances in the recent past. On the other hand, their past record against the Aussies in England and their recent heroics against the Kiwis on the home soil can boost England's morale. But at the end of the day, to win an Ashes series of this magnanimity, the tough should get going as the going gets tough!

CHAPTER TWENTY-SIX

AWAITING CHAMPION OF CHAMPIONS

(Week ending June 10, 2017)

The Champions Trophy is back! This 2017 edition is unique in the sense, Bangladesh has managed to make a dramatic entry at the expense of the West Indies, once world leaders in the 50 over format. We will not get to see them around this time, mainly riddled with their own inconsistencies as well as internal politics. They are undoubtedly the unstoppables and the most unpredictable – and this is what has exactly kept them at bay this time around. Every cricket lover will surely and sorely miss the presence of the Calypso charmers and it is a pity that their absence has taken the sheen out this otherwise exciting competition.

As the name itself suggests, this tournament belongs to Champion sides and to win, a team has to be a 'champion of champions'. As always, there are two groups of four teams each and the top two from each group make it to the semi-finals. This leaves teams with no choice but to win atleast two games in the group stage, especially the first match to reduce the pressure in the remaining two. But ofcourse, skill set is required to be a worthy team and this is brought in by the players. South Africa looks the team in form. But thanks to the chokers tag or the ability to constantly succumb under pressure, South Africa has never been able to win a major ICC title. If they can handle that out, they will be justified in expecting to lift the trophy, especially the last one for AB De Villiers.

India, the defending champions are oozing with confidence. The most equipped in all departments and with Dhoni there to guide Kohli and the young brigade, the team looks most formidable. Under Kohli, the team will like to put aside old performance and keep winning. Their ODI performance of late hasn't been great but with the current team playing to their ability, there is no stopping them. Looking into the warm up games and the marquee opening clash with Pakistan where India's neighbours were decimated to being silent spectators by a rampaging India, the team can only look forward to more laurels in the remaining matches. Semi-finals may be the only check point where India need to rely on their abilities and do the basics right, especially whilst batting. A good start is bound to snowball into a giant total, unsurpassable by any opponent with the kind of pace attack they have in these typical English conditions. It is after a long time that the young stars of Team India have stood up for the team's cause and India have been fortunate to find their biggest short format treasure in Hardik Pandya who is obsessed with playing good cricket and is a man possessed on the field, be it batting, fielding or bowling. Just watch out for him and old war horse, Yuvraj Singh!

Australia, proud about its good bench strength has always come up with an ace up it's sleeve during big matches. They have been fortunate by getting off the hook against New Zealand in their opening match, thanks to good rain at a bad time. This salvaged point may ensure they reach semi-finals by hook or crook. Once there, they are a different team and ofcourse, the team to watch and beware of. Undoubtedly, the best batting team in the short format, they are capable of chasing any total and with their mixture of deceitful bowlers, are capable of defending any total. Batting or struggling to bat against genuine spinners may be their main obstacle on their way to possible glory. They will do well to be cautious against the Asian teams like India, Bangladesh or Srilanka. Having lost their first match to India, Pakistan may not get the opportunity to be a part of the last four and have a go at Australia, especially considering they have to overcome two strong teams in Srilanka and South Africa.

In one corner and unnoticed is England, the hosts. It's abilities need no introduction when it comes to playing in home conditions at this time of the year. They have already shown their form and class by chasing a mammoth total of over 300 effortlessly against Bangladesh in their opening match. Any team which is dreaming of overcoming England here has to play out of it's teeth and that is what is Champions Trophy all about. Such is England's batting class right now, that a few of their top batsmen are capable of scoring a quick ton even whilst half asleep. The biggest test and most exciting match in their Group will be their match against New Zealand which will decide not only their respective fate, going forward, but Australia's as well.

Two teams, Pakistan and Bangladesh look certain to miss out on the knock-out stage, having lost their respective opening matches and awaiting to play the remaining true in-form champions. The black horse of this competition is New Zealand who have always surprised everyone. With a strong initial batting line-up, they are capable of giving a run for their money to the other teams. If any team can quickly adapt to the English bowling conditions, it is New Zealand. Watch out for the Kiwis!

We miss dear West Indies. The champions trophy is not the same without them, the champions of exciting cricket. Let's sit back and enjoy the champions' cricket and let the best team win!

CHAPTER TWENTY-SEVEN

BANGLADESH CLINCH CHAMPIONS TROPHY BERTH

(Week ending June 27, 2015)

Bangladesh deservedly achieved their first ever ODI series win over India and clinched their slot in the 2017 Champions Trophy well in advance. This is the first time ever, a team like Bangladesh has had a dream run of this magnitude. Trouncing Zimbabwe 5-0 recently, followed by a 3-0 whitewash of Pakistan seems to have given them immense confidence of whacking India 2-1. Such was their domination that they did not have to wait for the 3rd ODI to decide the winners. Bangladesh have been on a roll ever since they defeated England to make it to the world cup quarterfinals.

Honestly, India never knew what hit them and from which side. Ten home wins on the trot at home shows what a transformed side this Bangladesh eleven is, with each one of their players vying to make an invaluable contribution. In a stunning display of ruthless cricket, Bangladesh won key moments throughout the first two matches to ensure the momentum never ceased. Bowling out India twice itself is a major indication of the hosts' bowling domination. Suddenly, India's neighbours have come out with a handful of young and aspiring limited overs specialists in Mustafizur Rahman, Soumya Sarkar, Litton Das, etc., Simply, they were bursting with inspired performers with seniors like Mushfiqur Rahim and Shakib Al Hassan helping them. But they did chip in with their part too when it was needed.

After losing the first two matches, Dhoni had no choice, but to admit his men were just outplayed, toyed with and finally had to face the uphill task of avoiding a series whitewash. Though India has won 75% of their matches this season, this Bangladeshi jolt was never expected, especially after the dominating win over the neighbours in the recently concluded world cup match. Indian batsmen were given no time either to think or move their feet. Looking into their hapless position makes one wonder if this was the same batting unit which took India into the world cup semi-finals.

For Bangladesh, yet another star was born. Mustafizur Rahman, just 19 years old, bamboozled the Indians with his left arm pace, though with not much speed. In a record breaking show, Mustafizur became the first Bangladeshi to claim 5 wickets apiece in the first two matches, finishing the series with a 13 wicket haul, sharing the world record for this unique feat. The team support staff and management identifified Mustafizur's potential and fought hard to rope him into the T20 squad against Pakistan and the rest is in front of us to see. Yes, India always had problems with left arm pacers bowling over the wicket, but they were clearly bowled over this time around.

Bangladesh have clearly taken the cricketing world by storm and are here to stay. The message to the rest is, we are a transformed side and a tough nut to crack. They were clearly the better side in this series, having played well and executed their skills much better than the Indians. Looks like their knockout loss to India in the world cup has woken them up. The cricketing world may have been surprised, but Bangladesh were oozing with confidence as they knew their potential well. Selecting four pacers in the playing eleven for each of the first two ODI's seems to have surprised the Indians. This season has brought out the aggressive side of this well oiled Bangladeshi unit who have been underachieving for quite a long time and the Tigers have surely taken a big leap in international cricket in the last few months.

It is pathetic to see the Indian skipper claiming their side is tired and exhausted after too much cricket. It is a known fact India has been failing miserably in most of the international matches played immediately after the IPL in the recent years. It will be more appropriate to cite over confidence and lack of a serious approach on the Indians' part in this humiliating series loss. Of late, Team India has been grappling to identify a proper team coach and supporting staff unit. Rift in the team and dressing room discomforts too seem to be somewhat responsible to this poor show. For quite some time, India's team selection has been under a cloud, especially with the skipper repeatedly choosing not to utilise the bench strength fully inspite of a few regular non-performers getting chance after chance.

This loss has only seen Dhoni showering praise on individual capabilities of some of the team members, notwithstanding the end result. Yet again, his captaincy and team selection has come under scanner. Dhoni no longer seems to be the captain cool we all knew. First, he quit Test captaincy midway in a series in Australia sometime ago. This time, he has stopped short by offering to quit ODI captaincy if required. Instead of coming out with ideas to win matches, Dhoni seems to be ready with reasons for each and every defeat. Indian fans don't need frequent introspections. They need results and for this, the captain needs forward thinking. How can a team perform confidently under a captain with this mindset? He is expected to lead from the front, not leave from the front.

With much tougher overseas tours coming ahead, the question is, does this team has in it to achieve greater heights? We have been only seeing factors splitting the team. Nothing will change unless we see factors knitting the team. For Indian fans, this is a spineless display by such a talented bunch, boasting of their capabilities, only to fail miserably to lose to their neighbours, that too in familiar sub-continent conditions. This is a classic case of the Bangla Tiger mauling the asian giant!

CHAPTER TWENTY-EIGHT

SELECTION FOLLIES HURT INDIA

(Week ending August 09, 2014)

The current much anticipated India-England series is evenly balanced right now. This is a perfect reflection of two sides that have been struggling to register wins in Test cricket. While England has failed to win in around 10 Test matches before coming to this series, India's recent overseas record too has been quite unimpressive.

The first Test ended in a draw with players from both sides chipping in with timely contributions to ensure a draw for their respective sides. The historic Indian win at Lords ended their victory drought there, raising hopes of revival of Indian cricket abroad. Ishant shot to fame once again, only to become a victim to injuries in the next Test while Jadeja showed some heroics which eventually fizzled out in Southampton. Not surprisingly, India handed the 3rd Test on a platter to England in a spineless display, far from the commitment shown in the Lords Test, thanks mainly to dropped catches as well as players.

Indian batsmen not showing teeth in overseas conditions is not quite uncommon. The story was the same in this lost Test as well. A winning Team's batting always evolves around its openers. Though Murali Vijay showed form in patches, the story of Shikhar Dhawan is quite pathetic, raising serious doubts as to if he is the player who made a scintillating debut against the mighty Aussies a while ago. Looking back into his recent scores, it is extremely difficult to recall one stand out performance ever since he debuted. The current impression thrown around by Indian batting is that of a bunch of batsmen shining in patches with no purpose and in need of a sheet anchor.

What is Gautam Gambhir doing in the team idling on the bench? Sure, he was dropped for lack of form a few months ago. If Dhoni is rigid to persist only with Dhawan, then why pick Gambhir in the squad in the first place? If past performance is a non-indicator, the same currently applies to Dhawan as well. Dhawan's inability to handle the moving ball is surely eroding the confidence of the batsmen to follow, throwing up doubts in their minds. Kohli and Pujara too failing consistently and surprisingly is extending India's batting woes.

The temptation to play an extra batsman has ruined team India many a time. The extra batsman has never brought in the desired results. If 6 batsmen cannot make runs, can the 7th one make any difference? It is not the batsmen alone who can win a Test match. Whereas, 5 bowlers can be more effective where 4 bowlers cannot take 20 wickets. Very surprisingly, this has been one of the rare series where India is yet to play a genuine spinner and they are going into the 4th Test. Moeen Ali's career best 6 wicket haul in the second innings of the third Test is a proof of the current state of the Indian batting. This also throws up a question whether Ashwin would have been handy for India if he had got a chance. The Indian fielding too is below par and needs to transform.

The challenges currently being faced by India are more from within than from outside. Their batsmen, bowlers, fielders and the captain himself have to stand up. England too seems to have woken up after their Ashes drubbing with their skipper Cook back in business and Anderson shining away with the new ball. In addition, Ballance has been a thorn in India's flesh while Joe Root is proving to be the root cause of India's problems with his consistency. Anderson's let off from the recent enquiry will mean he will continue to play in this series giving India sleepless nights.

Inspite of all this, if ever India can win a series in England, this is the best chance. With Ishant injured and Bhuvi in doubt, India have their task cut out. This is the time for Gambhir and Ashwin to step in. But will skipper Dhoni step out of his rigid and defensive approach to make bold changes which can make a difference to the team's fortunes? Indian batsmen, including their seniors need to rally around young Ajinkya Rahane, their man in form. Let's hope Dhoni will learn from the earlier selection follies atleast now. It's time to see if Old Trafford will bring out a new story!

CHAPTER TWENTY-NINE

THE GABBA IS FINALLY BREACHED

(Week ending January 23, 2021)

Team India came to the Gabba, Brisbane to play the deciding 4th Test with nine down to injuries, but completely healed from the Adelaide debacle, thanks to the Melbourne win and the famous Sydney draw. A team which finished the first Test batting with a miserable 36 for 9 to go one down in the series had a huge uphill and impossible task on hand. India's never say die attitude and the heroics in the last couple of weeks ensured they rewrote history by scripting a nerve wracking chase to confine the Aussies to only their second loss on this ground in the last 32 years. It was the West Indies who last beat the Kangaroos here way back in 1988 and arguably, they were the only team who were competent enough to do it then in the 80's.

Excepting Pujara's stubborn resistance and his able support to first Gill and then to Pant, the other two senior batsmen, Rohit and Rahane failed to rise to the occasion here. This will surely be one of the India-Australia Tests to be remembered for centuries to come after the epic Kolkata win almost a couple of decades ago. If India's fortunes on the pitch took a plunge before that comeback script then, it was India's woes off the field this time around. With a combined experience of only 4 Tests, the pace quartet laid the foundation for India in style. No one gave a chance to the Indians before they arrived here and even last night, a draw appeared a huge achievement enabling India to retain the Border-Gavaskar Trophy. But the young brigade surely had different ideas and their own strategy. Probably a draw was never in their mind at all.

The progressive increase in the absence of the seniors throughout the series never deterred this bunch. They had nothing to lose except giving themselves an opportunity to ensure a long India career in whites respectively. Long after the emergence of fearless India under the leadership of Sourav Ganguly against this very same Aussies, a team which has seized every opportunity coming their way has shown that a new India is born again. Ganguly must be the happiest and proudest man watching this team display immense self-belief, positive attitude, character and temperament. Today, this Test win has destroyed the myth that the Aussies are unbeatable at the Gabba. The young Indians rose to the challenge and once again reaffirmed why Test cricket is so special and unique. This series win would have surely inspired 100's of millions of young Indians once again to take up cricket and that too as a career. In fact, this 2-1 victory has surely removed the shorter formats of the game from the limelight and confined them to the background for now, much to the pride of every Indian.

A two digit total in the beginning of an overseas series earlier would have made the players believe all is lost, eventually giving up without putting up a fight. But just to look at a few instances, it is stunning to see how this team has turned it's fortunes around throughout. In fact, the Aussies would have never got or will never get a better chance to have pocketed the series 4-0 after the battering they administered to India in Adelaide and more so, every match seeing a bunch of players, especially seniors getting sidelined one after the other due to injuries. Every true cricket fan around the world will surely savour this inspirational comeback series win against all odds. Having begun playing Tests in 1932, Indian cricket has today come a long way and it is incredible considering how the shorter formats have played a spoilsport many a time to the longest version of the game. This is India's third highest ever successful chase in the 4th innings of a Test match and only the first ever above 300 chase in Australia. With this, they have won against the Aussies in a chasing cause for the second time in Australia and for the fifth time overall.

The youngsters stunned the cricketing world with numerous stellar performances in all the 4 Tests with quite a few turning points. If Rahane had set the tone and lead from the front with his ton at Melbourne, it was the debutants and the Test cricket novices who took charge of delivering blow after blow to the Aussies. To begin with, it was the spare pace engine rising to the occasion. The batting achievements will stand up and has spoken volumes about the courage displayed, especially against the unchanged, power packed pace attack of the Aussies and the ever testing spin of Nathan Lyon. The batting has been sheer podium stuff with Gill and Pant turning the apples of the eye for Team India. Pant might have scored a huge ton in Sydney in the earlier tour, but surely, his consistent, timely and crucial knocks in succession nailed the final coffin on the Aussies' prospects.

Not just for their bowling, but one can only admire in awe, the record partnership between Washington Sundar and Shardul Thakur in the first innings of this Test. Surely, that was the turning point which ensured the Aussie lead was kept to the minimum, thereby increasing the chances of a chase within 400 and the rest is history now. Inspite of the dismissals of Pujara and Mayank Aggarwal at a crucial juncture, the Indian dressing room was quite cool, knowing well the boys will deliver this time, unlike on most of the previous occasions in a 4th inning chase. One can now say with confidence that players like Gill, Pant, Sundar, Shardul, Siraj, Saini and Natarajan have arrived and have well cemented their place on the Indian bench. The return of seniors in the near future will surely be a cause for dilemma for the selectors but this young bunch cannot be brushed under the carpet going forward in the long run. It is also great to note that Gill was the highest scorer for India for the series till the last hour of the match before Pant rightfully overtook him to emerge with the highest total. This is the new Indian cricket now.

It is a matter of pride that this team has retained the prestigious trophy not just with a draw, but with a record 4th Test win at Brisbane as well as the much deserved repeat series win in Australia and will rightfully hold their it's head high. Way back in Kolkata, the BCCI President Sourav Ganguly must be surely smiling and recalling his historic trips down under. Way back in 1971, a young batsman who debuted for India in the West Indies made history, taking the cricketing world by storm and holding fort of the Indian batting for a couple of decades thereafter. That cricketing legend, Sunil Gavaskar will surely be elated today not only to see the Border-Gavaskar Trophy retained by India, but with his prediction of a 2-1 series win for India coming true.

The new gen team India has arrived. Every Indian fan will today vouch that Indian cricket's future is surely in safe hands now.

CHAPTER THIRTY

DINESH KARTHIK WOULD HAVE BEEN A VALUE ADD (World Cup 2011)

The only time India won the cricket world cup was in 1983. Ever since that epochal moment, the Cup has been elusive for Team India, which has otherwise achieved almost everything on the cricket field. And with the 2011 World Cup round the corner, every Indian cricket fan is hoping the nation's dream of an encore would come true this time around. We have dethroned Australia from the No.1 spot in Test rankings but have proved no match to their winning the World Cup four times, including three in a row.

India's World Cup campaign would revolve around a team that has batsmen who can bowl and bowlers who can bat. The team can actually boast of more bowlers than batsmen. No back-up wicket-keeper for Mahendra Singh Dhoniand the absence of one extra batsman in the squad will pose uncomfortable questions ahead of the showpiece tournament.

The selectors could have been better off picking Dinesh Karthik instead of one of the spinners. It would have given the team the option of having an extra keeper, extra opener/batsman and also a capable fielder sans gloves. Moreover, Karthik is a cool headed cricketer and has ample experience behind him.

The 15-man squad comprises seven bowlers and seven batsmen with Dhoni undoubtedly qualifying more as a batsman, making the total batsmen to eight. Of the batsmen on hand, at least five can roll their arms over should the need be there, and almost all five have at times performed like frontline bowlers. In fact, this ensures we have 12 available bowling options. Perhaps, India will be the only team which has such a combination in a squad of 15.

By picking three spinners, the selectors have just added ammunition which may remain unused. The selectors have taken a gamble in going for an extra spinner at the cost of an additional batting option. India will be going into the World Cup with the uncomforting truth that their batting looked suspect on the recent tour of South Africa. Of course, it helps that the mega event will be played in the sub-continent.

Then there are fitness concerns to the batting department with three potential openers in Sachin Tendulkar, Virender Sehwag and Gautam Gambhir all nursing injuries. God forbid, if one or two of them either do not recover in time or aggravate their injury! We do not have a plan B.

The team appears to have the wherewithal to win the World Cup. Tendulkar will be playing his 6th World Cup. Just like Team India post 1983, the maestro has achieved everything on the field, save for being part of a World Cup-winning side. He wants to win it this time for his team and his team wants to win it for him. Let's pray both of them succeed.

Now that the squad is picked, there is no looking back. This isn't the time to moan. The selectors have done their job and let's hope the campaign turns out to be a champagne moment for all of us.

On the other hand, Kohli has played a big hand in India's ODI success in the last one year. He was India's best bet and if cricket had an award for the "Best & Promising Youngster", Kohli would have no serious contest to bag the honours. His tenure at the wicket always gives the impression that he is one of the seniors with a specific purpose of not only stabilizing the innings, but also dominating the bowling attack with disdain.

Fortunately for Dhoni, despite the handicap of having one batsman less in the squad, he can afford different permutations and combinations in the batting line-up, thanks to these two.

India is one of the most formidable batting outfits not only due to the individual talents, but also due to the various options it has at its command. If Kohli gives an extra 30 runs due to his batting, Raina is sure to cut the opposition total by at least 30 runs through his brilliance on the field. Both are match winners in their own right and will surely cash in on any slip by Yuvraj or Pathan. If Dhoni too returns to form, no total will appear small to chase.

Dhoni is a shrewd captain and knows how to play his cards. He also knows Indian middle order is like a piece of shining glass that needs to be handled with care.

CHAPTER THIRTY-ONE

CRICKETING STARS AND FLUCTUATING FORTUNES

(Week ending February 25, 2012)

The last few days of international cricket witnessed mixed results, career making and career breaking moments and also proved to be payback time for the English team in their ODI series against the Pakistanis. The ongoing CB Series is tantalisingly poised with India sliding down the points table after being on top for some time. But the top news of the week is the stunning exclusion of the veteran Ricky Ponting from the Australian ODI side and the emergence of the South African star Richard Levi in the shortest format of the game, respectively.

Ricky Ponting, a man who has represented the Kangaroos 375 times in ODI's, had to face this day after failing to reach double digit score in five consecutive matches. The previous world cup loss to India saw him quitting as the Aussie ODI skipper after representing his country in five world cup campaigns, three of them successful with two of them as skipper. Though he proved a point in the recently concluded Test series against India by scoring a double century, a century and three fifties with a stunning average of over 100, the almost certain end to his ODI career clearly indicates the forward thinking of the Australian Cricket Board. With age catching up fast with Ponting, Australia's eyes and plans are on the 2015 world cup to be played on their home soil and they are bent on building a team meant to bring the world cup back home. A much admired and respected Test batsman, Ponting's ODI achievements are of equal significance, having scored 13,704 career runs at an average of 42.03 accompanied by 30 hundreds and 80 fifties. It will take years before the Aussies fill the void created by Ponting's absence.

Whilst a glittering Australian ODI career seems to have come to an end, a star was born for South Africa in the neighbouring New Zealand in the form of Richard Levi. Playing in only his second T20 for his country, Levi tore apart the Kiwi attack and made a mockery of the high target the

Proteas were set. The Kiwis were stunned to witness his blitzkrieg in a hurricane 100 reached just off 45 balls. His unconquered 117 was studded with 13 sixes, a record for T20 internationals and 5 fours. In other words, his boundaries alone missed a 100 narrowly as they got him 98 runs. His match winning knock made him the first South African to get a T20 100 and also fetched him most runs through boundaries alone in a T20 international. His century is also the fastest in T20's till date, beating the earlier record held jointly by both Chris Gayle of West Indies and Brendon McCullum of New Zealand. He also went on to hit 13 huge audacious sixes to brush aside the previous record of 10 sixes held by Chris Gayle. His emergence has undoubtedly induced a welcome flavour to T20 cricket, especially to the South African side, but it is unfortunate he is not a part of his team set to play a 3 match ODI series against the Kiwis. He was not a part of the original squad and his whirlwind knock could not succeed in changing the selectors' mind who decided to stick to the original 14, thereby reaffirming their faith in them. Though the team is overflowing with immense batting strength at present with the likes of Graeme Smith, Kallis, Amla and De Villiers, it would have given them added options, especially if the series does not unfold with a win on expected lines. For the time being, Levi will be confined to the four walls of T20 cricket and will remain branded as a T20 specialist, what with the T20 world cup around the corner during the second half of the year. Till then, he will return home to do domestic duties. For the time being, Proteas' loss is Kiwis' gain.

Far away, in the middle-east, it was time for sweet revenge for the English team. Their in- form skipper led from front in the first three matches to wrap up the series at the end of the third match. The fourth match, though saw a good partnerhip from the Pakistan opening pair, ended on the prevailing lines with England winning it and making a clean sweep of the series 4-0. None gave them a chance of doing this when the series began. But thanks to mainly three men, Finn in bowling and Cook and Pietersen in batting respectively, England could dominate their opponents without troubling their remaining players much for any additional contributions. For Pakistan, unlike the Test series, it was abject surrender by both their batsmen as well as their bowlers.

A see-saw battle is on in the CB Series in Australia. Just a week ago, India were on top of the leader board. Successive defeats in two matches ensured they were placed at the bottom of the table. All within a few days. India is undoubtedly suffering from loss of form and absence of confidence which is currently at it's lowest ebb. The question is, with the current form and turmoils off the field like players' feud, rotation policy and arrogant selection policies, does the team really deserve to be in the finals with the Kangaroos and the Lankan Tigers playing excellent cricket on the other hand? India's bowling at the death has been thoroughly and repeatedly exposed. The batsmen are suffering from self-imposed trauma and destruction. The famed batting line-up has produced miserable knocks till date. Only three of the batsmen, Kohli, Gambhir and Dhoni have managed reasonable knocks whilst Sachin (90 off five innings), Rohit Sharma (79 off five innings, Sehwag (30 off three innings) and Raina (134 off six innings) have all made laughing stocks of themselves respectively. The absence of Dhoni in the match against the Lankans due to the one match ban did not help the team's cause either. India' inability to wrap up the tail has been a perennial problem for long and they do not seem to find a way out. They are currently struggling with team combination and are a confused lot with the so called rotation policy. India need to win both their remaining matches, which, if it happens, will be called a miracle. With the current form and frame of mind, it is highly unlikely. But cricket has always remained a funny game. Let's wait and watch. Only the finalists will tell!

The South Africans have pulled off a stunner to win the third T20 by 3 runs and thereby, the T20 series 2-0. The Kiwis will be baffled, having failed to score 10 off last 12 balls with 6 wickets in hand! For these two teams, cricket is certainly a funny game.

CHAPTER THIRTY-TWO

CUP ASPIRANTS FACE STERNER TESTS

(Week ending September 29, 2012)

The first round of the T20 world cup went the expected way. Very few matches were closely fought and quite a few turned out one sided affairs. However, with the super 8 finalised and split into two groups, the forthcoming matches are expected to see a keen tussle between the bat and the ball. Unlike earlier, there are no favourites at this stage as all the teams are more or less of the same standard and the difference between the winners and the losers will only be hair's breadth.

On individuals front, there were very few notable performances like Brendon McCullum's 72 ball 123, Imran Nazir's 36 ball 72, both against the hapless Bangladesh respectively and Shakib Al Hasan's 84 against Pakistan. On the bowling front, Ajanta Mendis ripped through Zimbabwe with a T20 international bowling record of 6 for 8 followed by Harbhajan's dream comeback spell of 4 for 12 against the mighty England. Having been kept out of the team for more than a year, Bhajji has now cemented his place for the future matches, especially the next big game against the Aussies as he savours playing against them.

Though McCullum hit a whirlwind century, the highest in T20 internationals to date, Imran Nazir's 72 will be rated much higher not only for it's timing but as it also came under heavy pressure. Pakistan not only needed to win, but also had to accomplish a higher net run rate to keep their chances alive. Nazir's blitzkrieg resulted in Pakistan's highest successful T20 international chase and proved he is a perfect fit for T20 cricket. Shakib Al Hasan's heroics were not enough as the bowlers let their team down which eventually ensured Bangladesh too followed the minnows by heading home. With this knock, however, he has justified his no.1 allrounder ranking in Tests as well as ODI's.

Though Mendis' spell against the minnows Zimbabweans was a record, Harbhajan's performance was of more significance to him as well India and it came out of the blue. Firstly, he never expected a national recall and was playing county cricket for Essex far away. Fortune smiled on him when he was picked in the eleven against England and he seized the opportunity. From his body language, it is evident he is bent on giving testing times for rival teams.

Though the T20 rankings are meaningless when the world cup is on, India's win against England enabled them jump four places to third rank. The week also saw West Indies fall four places to eighth, England slip to second rank and South Africa clinch the first. This world cup is certainly bound to result in re-arrangement of the rankings.

Enter second round, the teams know they cannot afford to lose more than one match. Each match is set to be a thriller and many close finishes are round the corner. The big boys have their task cut out and team selection will be a delicate issue for teams to grapple with as no team is a favourite henceforth.

International cricket will not see the coolest of umpires, Simon Taufel, a perfectionist, in action any more. Having umpired 74 Tests and 174 ODI's, he will retire to spend time with his family. Let us wish him good luck and happier times!

CHAPTER THIRTY-THREE

ENGLAND DEPRIVED OF A RARE FEAT

(Week ending July 07, 2012)

In the current ODI series against Australia, England will rue the washed out third ODI, especially after winning the first two ODI's. Though they can't lose the series now, their hopes of becoming the no.1 ranked ODI side evaporated in thin air as they can no longer win the series 5-0. Only this would have ensured they toppled the current leaders Australia. With this, they have forfeited the chance to become the first international team to top all three formats of the game as they already head the Test and T20 formats respectively.

The remaining two ODI's will not see the English offie Graeme Swann in action due to a sore elbow. This is a part of the team management's injury management plan to keep him fit for the oncoming marquee series against South Africa. These two matches will also most probably see Chris Woakes and James Tredwell in action for England. Tredwell who last played for England during the 2011 World Cup is picked as Swann's replacement whilst fast bowler Woakes has already been with the squad as cover and will remain so for the last two matches.

Sri Lanka's Kumar Sangakkara not only saved his team from the ingnonimity of defeat in the second Test against Pakistan, but also reclaimed the no.1 ICC Test ranking for batsmen in style pushing behind Shivnaraine Chanderpaul in the process. This ensured Sri Lanka go into the third Test 1-0, knowing very well they can now not lose the series. Though he missed the opportunity to score a double hundred twice in succession by scoring an unbeaten 199 in the first and 192 in the second respectively, he won many a heart and in the process, also overtook Sunil Gavaskar of India as the highest run scorer against Pakistan.

The bowling rankings continue to be headed by Dale Steyn of South Africa closely followed by Saeed Ajmal of Pakistan. Junaid Khan and Abdur Rehman, both of Pakistan, gained significant jumps in the rankings, thanks to their recent respective five wicket hauls against Sri Lanka.

After having won both the T20's played in the USA against the Kiwis convincingly, West Indies now go into the ODI series confidently. Whilst the Windies are ranked eighth, New Zealand are ranked just slightly above at seventh. Though West Indies are packed with their in-form local heroes, the series is set to be closely fought. Their recent 2-2 in a five match series against the no.1 ranked Kangaroos will keep the Windies in good stead and they will certainly take heart from this feat. But the subsequent 0-2 loss to England has exposed their inconsistency in this form of the game and will give ample confidence to the Kiwis. The series is sure to offer spectators and television viewers, their money's worth.

Back in the sub-continent, India announced their 15 man squad for their forthcoming tour of Sri Lanka. They are set to play 5 ODI's and one T20. Whilst Virender Sehwag and Zaheer khan have returned to the team after injury lay offs, their star batsman Sachin Tendulkar has opted to sit out, thereby giving an opportunity to the recent IPL star Ajinkya Rahane who consistently did well. Tendulkar has been recently nominated to the Indian Parliament and is currently a sitting MP.

CHAPTER THIRTY-FOUR

EXPERIENCE AND YOUTH RESCUE PAKISTAN

(Week ending February 16, 2013)

The second Test between South Africa and Pakistan is currently underway. The pitch at Cape Town was dry and different from the one for the first Test. But it seems it has no impact on the fortunes as Pakistan yet again had no answer to the Proteas' pace attack, having conceded four wickets before lunch on the first morning. It looks like the problem is with the batsmen's mindset and this match too will probably not go into the fifth day, barring a miracle by the visitors' batsmen in the second outing. With skipper Misbah too woefully out of form, the team's batting fortunes depended on veteran Younis Khan and Asad Shafiq, both of whom scripted an excellent recovery subsequently with well deserved respective centuries.

With Pakistan's ace pace bowler Junaid Khan out due to a thigh injury, the visitors may find it very tough to run through the Proteas' batting line-up. Mohammed Irfan, coming from a dream spell of 7 for 40 in the practice game, has made his Test debut and will have his task cut out. With their openers already struggling, Pakistan have lost the trick in playing Nasir Jamshed suffering from an ankle injury who failed yet again.

Going into the third T20, the New Zealand-England series was locked 1-1. England's fine run and victory margin in the first match triggered possibilities of an English riot. But McCullum's men bounced back in style with himself leading from the front with a fluent 74. New Zealand's top three batsmen, especially Guptill, are in fine form and this should give them an edge in the decider. The English bowling attack though, will surely give the visitors a glimmer of hope. The return to form of some of the hitherto non-performing stars from either side like Ross Taylor or Finn may make all the difference to the winning side. The Kiwis would have surely gained confidence after having beaten England in the previous match after six consecutive T20 losses since 2007.

Back in Australia, the West Indies ended their tour on a high note inspite of getting whitewashed in the 5 match ODI series by winning the lone T20 match. It was a very special and historic occasion for the Windies as they had last beaten the Aussies in Australia in any format 16 years ago. The ODI series earlier saw the Windies failing to capitalise on many a winning situation. All centuries scored by their batsmen ended up in the losing cause. Chris Gayle was the biggest disappointment and his disappointing show was mainly responsible for their humiliating defeats.

Come the lone T20 match and the Windies who are ever shrewd in this format kept their prestige intact. The Aussies die not field their prime team. But this doesn't matter in an international match. The hosts were thoroughly outclassed thanks to Johnson Charles' 57 and Kieron Pollard's 3 wicket haul following his breezy and useful knock with the bat. Sunil Narine too chipped in with a miserly spell claiming two wickets.

The women's world cup finals will see the West Indies play Australia on Sunday. The Aussies' surprise loss to the Windies and expected win over England respectively in the super six gifted the Windies a finals spot and devastated England!

CHAPTER THIRTY-FIVE

FLUCTUATING CRICKETING FORTUNES

(Week ending May 05, 2012)

It is time for England to rejoice again. They will be keenly looking forward to their forthcoming home encounters against the not so good looking West Indies. England are set to regain their lost pride and retain their no.1 slot at the end of this series. Their forgettable recent Test performances against Pakistan and Sri Lanka respectively will soon be a thing of the past. On the other hand, the West Indies are straight from a home drubbing received in the hands of the Aussies. The Windies are set to play 3 Tests, 3 ODI's and a lone T20 in England.

In what is set to be a less than a month's tour, the visitors are a depleted side with a no. of changes in their ranks. The inclusion of uncapped fast bowler Shannon Gabriel and Assad Fudadin may not help the visitors much as they have chosen to drop 3 of their tested Test cricketers Bishoo, Brathwaite and Carlton Baugh respectively. The only consolation will be the recalling of Denesh Ramdin, the wicketkeeper and Marlon Samuels who is expected to strengthen their middle order. However, the good news for them is that Chris Gayle is set to join them for the ODI series after a much awaited truce with the West Indies Board to end his year long exile from donning the national colours. Failing to make it to the Test series due to a delayed settlement, Gayle went on to forfeit his T20 contract with Somerset to prefer playing for the country. One can now expect the ODI series to be a well fought one, thanks mainly to the presence of Gayle though the Test series may not bring any smiles in the Windies dressing room.

Coming to the team and individual cricket rankings, Australia have regained some lost ground by moving to the third position in the ICC Test ranking after beating the Windies 2-0 in the three match series. In the process, India, the top ranked exactly a year ago, have now been pushed to the fourth position. Though England lead the rankings, they share points(116) with South Africa and a series win over the Windies will ensure they will continue to cling to this position for some more time to come. India needs to undergo a long rebuilding process if they are having any dreams or hopes of making it to the top again in the near future. Fortunately, they will not be playing outside the sub-continent which will ensure they will atleast not slide further down the table.

It is not surprising to see Shivnaraine Chanderpaul deservedly regain the no.1 Test batsman rank. His performance in the recently concluded series against the Aussies was a one man show in a losing cause. His consistent form proved a thorn in the flesh for the powerful Aussie attack. Undoubtedly, he is one of the few batsmen in Test cricket today who puts a price on his wicket. A tough nut to crack, his determination and commitment whilst at the crease puts him on a high pedestal. His clawing back to no.1 rank is no mean achievement, considering he had to leapfrog the renowned South African duo of AB de Villiers and Jacques Kallis. With no Indian in the top 20 list and not much of international cricket being played, other batsmen who moved up the ladder during the week are Ed Cowan, David Warner and Matthew Wade.

On the bowling front, South African Dale Steyn is still fittingly leading the pack, closely followed by Pakistan's Saeed Ajmal and James Anderson of England. With Anderson being a doubtful starter for the oncoming series against the West Indies, we may not see him improve his rank in the near future. The rest of the bowlers who managed to gain places are Kemar Roach and Shane Shillingford of the West Indies and Nathan Lyon and Michael Clarke of Australia. Clarke's surprising leap is due to his five wicket haul in the third Test against the West Indies. Inspite of India's recent poor showing, Zaheer Khan and Pragyan Ojha are amongst the few who have maintained their existing rankings respectively.

With the IPL entering it's last leg, Delhi Daredevils have bulldozed their way to the top of the points table closely followed by Kolkata Knight Riders. Pune Warriors are languishing at the bottom half of the table, slightly better off than the lowest placed Deccan Chargers in whose hands they tasted successive defeats. The rest are sandwiched in between, standing a chance of making it to the last four. The biggest disappointment has been the winners of the previous two editions, Chennai Super Kings. IPL has seen them bounce back always and may be this IPL is no exception.

Whether it is international cricket or IPL, teams or individuals, the race for supremacy is always on!

CHAPTER THIRTY-SIX

CAN RAINA TRANSLATE POTENTIAL TO PERFORMANCE?

Suresh Raina came into the Indian team with high expectations – a talented and multi-skilled player. A player with the potential to turnaround a match with his ability to hit long and hard, chip in with a few productive overs and be world class as a fielder. In that respect, he was expected to follow in the footsteps of another talented left-hander, Yuvraj Singh.

Despite getting branded as a limited overs specialist, Raina distinguished himself quickly by cracking a hundred on his Test debut. In the recent world cup, he upstaged Yusuf Pathan to cement his place in the do-or-die matches later in the tournament. With players like Virat Kohli and Yuvraj justifying their inclusions in the playing eleven, Raina had to bide his time. And when he finally got his chance, he grabbed it gleefully. His unbeaten knocks of 34 and 36 against Australia and Pakistanrespectively stand out as among the best world cup knocks by an Indian to power the team into the knockout stages.

Then coach of the then Indian team, Gary Kirsten put things in perspective: "He pretty much won the world cup for us with that knock against the Australians in the quarter-finals. He had just played one game and then he went on and played the most responsible, mature knock and won us the game. For me, that was really a combination of years of making mistakes but learning along the way."

However, there is a question mark over Raina's technique against short-pitched balls. And unless that flaw is corrected, the left-hander cannot hope to command a place in the Indian Test team.

Though his first stint as Team IndiaODI skipper on a tour to Zimbabweproved disastrous, he led a young brigade to a 3-2 win in the ODI series against the West Indies. However, his batting has been a let down in the Caribbean, more often than not, succumbing to poor shot selection. Raina andRohit Sharma carried a huge responsibility on their shoulders to prop an inexperienced batting line-up, but the skipper's failure placed a heavy burden on Rohit, who rose to the occasion by emerging as man of the series.

Raina's overall international record is quite mediocre as he scored just two half centuries from seven Tests after his sparkling debut, and in 119 ODI's, he has three hundreds and a batting average of just 34.

Heavyweights like Sachin Tendulkar, Rahul Dravid and VVS Laxmanare on the threshold of bidding their international careers adieu. Their exits will leave a vacuum in the Indian middle order. It's imperative that someone like Raina, who has been with the Indian team for around six years now to raise the bar and translate his potential into consistent performances.

CHAPTER THIRTY-SEVEN

GRIPPING CONTESTS ROUND THE CORNER

(Week ending February 02, 2013)

Pakistan's current tour of South Africa will be their biggest test in the recent times, especially having had a mixed bag of results in the last year or so. This tour is expected to test their batting as well as bowling firepower equally. They will play 3 Tests, 2 T20's and 5 ODI's in this long and grinding tour with the first Test slated to start on February 01, 2013. Graeme Smith is set to create history by becoming the first to lead a Test team for the 100th time, having lead the Proteas 98 times and the World XI once before. For the hosts, Robin Peterson who has been declared fit may still not find a place in the eleven if the team picks an all-pace attack.

Pakistan received the first blow as their opener Taufeeq Umar is being sent back as he failed to recover from a leg injury and is to be replaced by Imran Farhat. Inspite of having four quickies in the squad, the Pakistan team has requested the Board for reinforcements. As a result, Tanvir Ahmed and Rahat Ali are expected to join the team before the first Test. Seniors Umar Gul and Junaid Khan will guide and motivate the remaining four uncapped pacers on the typical fast and bouncy wickets. This is the best chance for the Pakistani quickies to rattle the hosts' batting line-up as these wickets suit them also equally well.

Down under, the Aussies are set to play 5 ODI's and a lone T20 against the West Indies before they embark on their all-important Test tour of India. Having managed to level the ODI series 2-2 and lose the T20 series 0-2 against Sri Lanka at home, the Kangaroos seem to be struggling to find the right combination in the shorter formats. Their star opener David Warner is out with a broken finger and is not likely to make the Indian trip either. The West Indies who are the reigning T20 champions are always a tough nut to crack when it comes to ODI's. While James Faulkner and Usman Khawaja have come in for injured Moises Henriques and David Warner respectively for Australia, Ramnaresh Sarwan is a case of welcome return to the Windies squad after a long hiatus and some legal action.

Currently, the Windies are ranked seventh in the ODI's, having lost their last ODI series 2-3 to Bangladesh. One good thing with the current squad is, it is a perfect mix of youth and experience and they are coming into this tour straight from the Caribbean T20. The last time these two played an ODI series, they drew 2-2. An interesting, but not surprising fact is that the West Indies last won an ODI series in Australia in 1992. Their last ODI victory here came 13 ODI's ago, in 1997. Their fate this time around wrests in the hands of players like Chris Gayle, Kieron Pollard and Sunil Narine.

Team India is now receiving the long awaited rest after a much awaited ODI series victory over England. They will take on Australia later this month in a 4 Test battle at home. The series will be gripping and skipper Dhoni will be looking forward to gripping and turning wickets to restore some home pride!

CHAPTER THIRTY-EIGHT

INDIA AND DHAWAN CREATE HISTORY

(Week ending March 26, 2013)

The third Test between New Zealand and England has begun in Auckland and it promises a nail-biting contest as England look to cement their no.2 Test spot by winning this match and the series while the Kiwis are desperately looking for a first series win over England since 1999. England's hopes, unfortunately, have received a jolt just before the start with their star batsmen getting himself ruled out for this Test as well as the forthcoming IPL due to a knee injury. This means the England batting will yet again depend on their ever reliable skipper Cook, Compton and Jonathan Trott to ensure they pull the rug from under the hosts' feet like they did in the last ODI recently.

With England set to host the Champions Trophy closely followed by Ashes at home and Graeme Swann also already an injury victim, they will dread the news of more injuries. Their prime bowler James Anderson is seen struggling with an yet to be diagnosed injury though he managed to bowl gruelling spells in the previous Tests.

The second Test between the hosts West Indies and Zimbabwe is going the expected way with off-spinner Shane Shillingford yet again proving to be Zimbabwe's nemesis. The visitors' inability to tackle his spin on bouncy wickets, Chris Gayle's striking his much awaited form and Marlon Samuel's all-round show seem to have taken the match away and it looks like this match too might be over within four days. Having skittled the visitors for only 175, the Windies' have gained a substantial lead.

With an unassailable 3-0 lead over the Aussies, India created history by registering 3 Test wins in a series against Australia for the first time which is likely to become 4-0 looking into the current form and confidence level of the Australians. Having got the much awaited break, Shikhar Dhawan too created history by registering the fastest ton by a debutant in Test cricket. His 187 is now also the highest debut ton by an Indian.

It is unfortunate he will be sitting out of the fourth Test due to a freak finger injury sustained whilst fielding. This means, India is facing another openers dilemma. Gambhir, the first choice to replace Dhawan was diagnosed with jaundice resulting in Raina joining the squad. But it looks like Ajinkya Rahane may get a nod ahead of Raina to earn his first Test cap.

Skipper Clarke may miss a Test for the first time due to his back injury. Vice-captain Shane Watson having returned, is likely to lead the team. It is surprising, just a week after contemplating quitting Test cricket, he is likely to captain Australia for the first time. Looking into the team's plight, Australia need both Watson and Clarke fit and firing to salvage some pride in the dead Test. With Mitchell Starc too flying home for a surgery, it looks like Mitchell Johnson may finally get a chance.

Pakistan did extremely well to win the fourth ODI to comeback in the series for the second time. Fine knocks by skipper Misbah and Imran Farhat followed Mohammed Irfan's two wickets in first two balls shattered the Proteas. This series will now be decided in the last ODI.

CHAPTER THIRTY-NINE

INDIA AWAITS TO WELCOME IT'S HERO

(Week ending September 08, 2012)

Yuvraj Singh is looking forward to donning Indian colours once again this Saturday when they take on the Kiwis in the first T20 match. But the whole nation is more eagerly awaiting his return to international cricket. He is the undisputed hero for India in the shorter formats, having all along been a trusted and tested star. His heroics in the last ODI world cup were mainly responsible for India emerging the champions. His mere presence brings in an aura and his all-round abilities ensure he adds immense value to the team.

It is going to be a huge moment in his life when he steps into the field today as he has just won the biggest battle of his life against cancer. This T20 series will also give him enough confidence and get his rhythm back, going into the T20 world cup in Sri Lanka. The thought of playing again for the nation was the biggest motivational factor for him and it is evident from his commitment and his recent workouts and practice sessions at the National Cricket Academy in Bengaluru. Let us extend our best wishes to him.

Pakistan comprehensively beat the Aussies by 7 wickets in the first match of the T20 series and is expected to dominate the series. This defeat is the biggest for the Kangaroos in terms of balls remaining. If Aussies lose this series, they will probably be ranked 10th, lower than Ireland and this will surely be the most embarrassing moment in their cricketing history. As on date, even their skipper Bailey admits they will most likely return empty handed from the world cup.

Pakistan ODI skipper Misbah has been severely criticized for his tactics in their 1-2 loss to the Aussies in the just concluded ODI series. Being tied at 1-1, they lost the best chance to win a ODI series against the Aussies in 10 years. The skipper himself failed with the bat and this is his 3rd ODI series defeat in a row. Strange moves by him like sending Afridi to bat at no.3, and holding back Kamran Akmal to bat lower down the order were his tactical errors in batting while many felt the team just lacked aggression and self-belief.

Inspite of an early hiccup in it's chase in the 3rd ODI, South Africa was steered to safety by the half centurions Amla and De Villiers to win the match and thereby square the 5 match ODI series 2-2. After having lost the Test series earlier, this draw is a consolation for England, especially looking into the terrific form the Proteas had been in all along. In fact, this is only the second ODI defeat for England in the current year. Two things evident from this ODI match are the Proteas' confidence against this English team and England's inability to set defendable targets. With new permutations and combinations in the team coming into play, it may take some time for England to get back into it's groove.

India are set to get into T20 mood after the expected 2-0 win in the just concluded Test series against the Kiwis. For the first time, Sachin Tendulkar was seen struggling at home, getting out bowled thrice in succession. The little master must surely be strategizing for the next series!

CHAPTER FORTY

INDIA'S HOME REPUTATION AT STAKE

(Week ending December 15, 2012)

Sri Lanka began their typically long cricket tour down under comprising of 3 Tests, 5 ODI's and 2 T20's. Just before the first Test began, their skipper Mahela Jayawardane announced his decision to give up captaincy immediately after this tour. However, he will be assisting Angelo Mathews who is set to take over and will continue playing for his country. Knowing him and his determination well, we can look forward to atleast a couple of memorable knocks from him and a motivated performance from his boys. After having failed to regain the no.1 Test slot from the hands of the Proteas, the hosts Australia will be well aware of what they need to do this time around to climb up the rankings.

After rallying from 0-2 to level the 5 match ODI series, West Indies succumbed to some scintillating hitting from the Bangladesh batsmen as well as pressure from the local fans to trip in the deciding one-dayer to lose the Sahara Cup to the well deserving hosts, Bangladesh. The lone T20 resulted in a high scoring game with both teams indulging in some brutal hitting. However, Marlon Samuels' last over blitzkrieg resulting in 29 runs made all the difference between the two sides. Inspite of a dream start, the hosts failed to capitalize on the same when they found it tough to score boundaries in the second half of their innings, thanks to some shrewd and miserly bowling by Chris Gayle.

The Test series being played between India and England was set to be a revenge series for the hosts. After etching out a comfortable win in the first Test, it looked like a clean sweep for India. Winning the toss in the first three matches, getting tailor-made tracks which turned square, playing extra spinners, possessing a famed batting line-up always excelling in home conditions, etc., were all in vain in the hosts' quest for subsequent wins. The teams' roles changed with the visitors' batsmen piling up huge scores and their spinners repeatedly running through the hosts' batting line-up.

England are now leading the series 2-1, going into the fourth and final Test. A win for them or a draw here will ensure they win a Test series in India after 27 years.

India's preparations for each of the matches have been riddled with concerns for the pitch, team selection controversies, their policies and skipper Dhoni's failure to perform as well as to extract performance from his players. Though the selectors made some daring changes by removing Yuvraj, Zaheer and Harbhajan for the fourth Test and rewarded Ranji performers Ravindra Jadeja, Awana and Piyush Chawla, the team is still holding on to some of the regular non-performers and it is to be seen if this will affect their chances of winning. If the Mumbai Test had three spinners playing for India, the ongoing Nagpur Test has four spinners and only one speedster in the playing eleven. This move may or may not halt India's dwindling fortunes, but it confirms India's desperation to win this Test and level the series.

Another failure here in Nagpur may see a new Test skipper and new team combinations for India in the near future. They need to stay focused and get their basics right with a self-belief to wriggle out of this quagmire. Will they?

CHAPTER FORTY-ONE

IT'S ADVANTAGE, HOME CONDITIONS

(Week ending February 18, 2012)

The international cricket calendar is probably the most hectic this month. It is only the West Indies and Bangladesh who are cooling their heels at present with almost all other major teams flexing their muscles, the common factor being the visiting teams have been thoroughly exposed in all the series that were played ever since the dawn of the year 2012.

One notable feature at the end of 2011 has been the first ever historic Test win for Sri Lanka against the Proteas in South Africa. This came in the Durban Boxing Day Test though the Lankans went on to lose the 3 Test series 2-1. In the subsequent ODI series, the Lankans lost the first three matches but ended up successfully chasing over 300 runs in the last two ODI's to lose the ODI series 2-3. Inspite of these herculean efforts, their coach Geoff Marsh found himself sacked by the new Board on the team's return to the island, that too only into the 4th month of his two year contract whilst the captain, Dilshan, was also replaced by Mahela Jayawardene. The year also did not begin on the expected lines for the reigning no.1 Test team England and the former no.1 India respectively. Both were drubbed in alien conditions with Pakistan handing England a 3-0 defeat and India tasting a repeat of the 0-4 mauling they received from England in the hands of the rejuvenated Aussies with their captain Michael Clarke leading from the front with a breathtaking triple century and also helped by the return to form of Ponting and Hussey, the old warhorses. If the Aussies' pace attack was the nemesis for the famed Indian batting line-up, the spin attack of Pakistan turned out to be England's waterloo. One common thing between England and India is that for both of them, climbing to the no.1 slot was much easier than retaining the same. Whilst India gave away the top slot to England on a platter, England's dismal show in the gulf has now ensured the top spot may be up for grabs in the coming months. Many felt the current tour of India down under was their best chance to beat the Kangaroos on their backyard, but the continuous rigid approach of the Indian management has ensured their team had to face the ignonimity of 8 overseas defeats on the trot. Added to this, the much anticipated, but not happening 100th international 100 of Tendulkar seems to have shifted the focus as well as the priorities of the team.

The start of the ODI series after the Test debacle has brought forth completely different England and Indian teams respectively. Whilst England beat Pakistan in the initial two ODI's, India, with it's young guns, has begun it's CB Series campaign rather reasonably well, having lost only one match to Australia till now. With the third team Sri Lanka struggling to come to grips, probably due to their Board's financial crunch , it looks like India and Australia will be the likely finalists. The last match between India and Lanka ended in a tie, the 26th one in ODI's overall and the first between these subcontinent neighbours. If India emerge winners in this format, it will atleast be a consolation to their recent consistent dismal performances overseas.

A quick look at Zimbabwe's just concluded tour of New Zealand will reveal the results were on expected lines with the visitors failing to win any of the one-off Test, 3 ODI's or 2 T20's. The Kiwi bowling firepower was too hot for the Zims to handle and they must have surely felt relieved when the tour finally got over. The consistently inconsistent performances in all formats by certain teams clearly indicate they need to set standards and strive to achieve them to compete with the rest. The results so far in the beginning of the year have clearly gone only in one direction ie., the home teams emerging victorious, especially in Tests. The week was also witness to the first ever ODI played by Afghanistan against a full fledged ICC member, Pakistan. Though Pakistan won comfortably as expected, Afghanistan can take pride from the more than decent fight and resistance put up by them.

The much awaited tour of South Africa to New Zealand is round the corner. Fans can be assured of mouth watering contests ahead. With wickets and conditions favouring pace bowlers, both the teams, with their respective bowling armoury are bound to take advantage, making the matches closely fought affairs. There is ample cricket in store for viewers with 3 T20's to start with, followed by 3 ODI's and culminating in a 3 Test series. New Zealand, though had whitewashed Zimbabwe in the just concluded series, will find the going tough and their fortunes will depend on their batsmen coming good against quality South African attack.

To sum up, all the recent series, whether Tests or ODI's mostly have given undue advantage and desired results to the home teams. Though Pakistan played away from home, they won on home conditions, those akin to subcontinent. The Proteas' Test series win against Sri Lanka at home must have brought them ample joy as a home series win was long overdue, the last one being 4 years ago.

Wins are to be savoured, especially those which are home made!

CHAPTER FORTY-TWO

CAN CAPTAIN COOL HANDLE PAKISTANI HEAT?

(Week ending December 29, 2012)

The Indo-Pak cricketing ties are set to resume on Christmas day after a gap of many years with India hosting their neighbours in a battle of shorter formats. They both are set to play 2 T20's and 3 ODI's in a tour sandwiched between the just concluded India-England T20's and oncoming ODI series respectively. In the midst of the busy international schedule, this much awaited and sought after short tour has come at a time when Indian cricket looks in shambles, especially after the home drubbing received in the hands of England in the just concluded Test series.

The two match T20 series against England raised some hopes of revival of India's fortunes with a win for the hosts in the first match, thanks to comeback man Yuvraj Singh's all-round effort. The second match too was going in India's favour when Dhoni and Raina seemed to take the match beyond England's reach. Dhoni's refusal of an existing third run with the score at 168 for 5 off 18.3 overs saw him getting out the next ball. This resulted in India managing a meager 9 runs in the remaining 8 deliveries. Dhoni's over confidence in his abilities and vis-à-vis Raina's ensured England's target was always realistic and within reach. As it always happens post such goof ups in cricket, England deservingly won with a last ball six. A win here for India would have taken them to no.1 spot in T20's for the first time, but not for now, may be, next time!

Any form of cricket between India and Pakistan is always the ultimate to their respective fans. Though they have been meeting on and off in world cup matches, a series played between them anytime always evokes special interest. Just on the day Pakistan arrived in India, Sachin Tendulkar bid adieu to ODI's. This means Tendulkar will not be seen in action in the ODI's against Pakistan for the first time in more than two decades. Indian fans must be wondering if their team will cope with his absence and emerge winners.

The current Indian bowling attack looks toothless and their batsmen are woefully out of form. This is the most undesirable scenario, especially against a team like Pakistan. Post the world cup win, India has had a miserable run without any reprive and they are now at the fag end of 2012, facing the biggest test of their abilities. They might have played the worst cricket in the recent past, but failure to beat the arch rivals at home will never be accepted and will leave their fans fuming. Whereas, a win here will turn them into heroes from disappointing zeros.

While Tendulkar retired for India, Pakistan have not picked boom boom Afridi in the team for the first time. He is set to feature in the T20 matches and their ODI captain Misbah-ul-Haq is still hopeful Afridi might play the ODI's, thanks to a couple of noteworthy performances in domestic cricket. Both the teams will see a few young and budding cricketers in action and a player with a notable performance here is set to make it big in his career.

Looking into the teams' strengths and weaknesses and recent performances, India's confidence must be at a very low ebb. The pressure of playing Pakistan, that too at home, is bound to add to their problems. Moreover, Pakistan seem to be in good stead as they have a bowling strength they can boast of. On the other hand, the Indian bowlers, especially in the absence of Zaheer Khan, will find it an uphill task running through the Pakistani batting line-up. The Indian batsmen have been predictably failing in the recent past and with Saeed Ajmal around, they have their task cut out. However, two men who can take away the match from Pakistan are Sehwag and Yuvraj and India's fortune mainly wrests with them.

If India win this time around, they will be atoning for all their recent sins and by winning here, Pakistan will be avenging their repeated world cup losses to India. While Pakistan have a problem of plenty, Dhoni needs to make optimum use of his limited resources. Between these two teams, form or quality do not matter much as it will be mainly a battle of nerves!

CHAPTER FORTY-THREE

IT'S NOW SEE-SAW BATTLES TIME

(Week ending May 12, 2012)

IPL 5 is now entering the penultimate week and it is no wonder, considering the intensity of the competition, only the top 2 and bottom 2 places respectively are certainities. The table is currently led by Delhi Dare Devils, the most consistent team in this edition closely followed by Kolkata Knight Riders. On the other side, at the bottom are Pune Warriors, who disappointed after a bright start and the whipping boys of this IPL, Deccan Chargers.

Inspite of losing Kevin Pietersen at halfway stage, Delhi Daredevils have carried on with the same audacity against most teams barring their match against Kolkata Knight Riders where they tasted defeat after quite sometime in the tournament. This rare defeat can be attributed to the joint failure of their renowned openers Sehwag and David Warner. However, they came back strongly in their next match against the Deccan Chargers to regain the top spot with a stellar performance when they made mockery of a huge target of 188 runs to win by 9 wickets with almost 3 overs to spare. This, inspite of Sehwag failing yet again, was mainly due to Warner's hurricane 100. Sehwag is still run hungry after his recent feat of 5 consecutive fifties, the first in T20 cricket. For any team dreaming to conquer Delhi, they need to first overcome the twin hurdles of their opening firepower.

In Kolkata Knight Rider's case, it has been a one man show with their skipper leading from the front with consistent scores. It is necessary that the rest start rising to the occasion as sooner or later, the law of average is set to catch up with Gambhir . Yousuf Pathan has been a disappointment so far, but Gambhir is confident he will fire when it matters most.

With Delhi and Kolkata set to clinch the top two spots, the remaining two are up for grabs with five teams pinning their hopes with realistic chances. With each of these five teams having played most of their league fixtures and with only a very few remaining, none of them can afford a slip up at this stage. As seen earlier in this edition, many a match have turned out cliff hangers with fortunes of teams hinging on a single delivery. The winner of previous two editions, Chennai Super Kings scrapped through a nerve wracking low scoring tie against Rajasthan Royals to keep their slim hopes alive. As in the earlier editions, Chennai look like coming from behind in this edition too to grab a place in the last four. If Albie Morkel has been bailing out Chennai in the last few matches, it is Chris Gayle and A B de Villiers who have been performing the rescue act for Royal Challengers Bangalore.

This IPL has seen only a few individuals shining for most of the teams and it has been less of a team work. A few teams have also lost key players to injuries. Lasith Malinga is the only player who has managed his injuries well to successfully come back to become the highest wicket taker of this IPL till date. Some of the key players whose injuries have weakened their respective teams' prospects are Adam Gilchrist, Kevin Cooper, Kieron Pollard and Sachin Tendulkar. Teams like Mumbai Indians, Kings XI Punjab and Rajasthan Royals, though are capable of beating any team on their day, need to come out with much stronger performances in their remaining matches and cannot afford to lose any of these matches. With the going getting tough, the tough need to get going!

With Sourav Ganguly opting to sit out of his team's remaining three matches with a view to giving chances to budding youngsters, Pune Warriors will have a new skipper and will bring out some new faces. Having already forfeited their chances of progressing further and nothing to lose, it will be no surprise if Pune now find back their winning ways in the matches to come. According to team sources, Sourav Ganguly is expected to play the role of a mentor in the coming editions of IPL and this means we have already seen the last of Ganguly in an IPL playing XI.

Though teams are vying to get into the last four, the top two teams will get two shots on the final. One of the semi-finals will be between the top two with the winner going into the finals and the loser playing the winner of the other semi-final. In other words, the loser of one semi-final will perceive the second attempt as an additional chance whilst the winner of the other semi-final will find the second try as an additional hurdle. Therefore, if it is enough to enter the last four, it is beneficial to finish amongst the first two!

CHAPTER FORTY-FOUR

LANKAN LIONS LOSE CUP, BUT WIN HEARTS

(Week ending March 10, 2014)

It was extremely sad to watch the Sri Lankans fail to cross the final hurdle inspite of lion-hearted performances in the CB Series. The third and decisive final saw the Aussies suffer mid-innings hiccups to collapse dramatically and set up an easy target of 232 to the Lankans. The Lankan lions faltered in their chase but certainly won hearts for the spirited fight they put up throughout.

When the Sri Lankan team arrived in Australia to take part in the CB Series, none gave them a chance to progress to the finals. But their reinstated skipper Mahela Jayawardene, had different ideas. He scripted an amazing turnaround and inspite of the historic loss to the Indians, carried his team to the finals in a deserving manner. If the seniors in the team chipped in with timely contributions, the youngsters were in no way lagging behind. In fact, their more than consistent contributions were of much more significance than their seniors'. Sri Lanka has become richer by a couple of youngsters in Dinesh Chandimal and Lahiru Thirumanne. The way these two carried the Lankan batting is truly amazing and the Lankans are assured of two bright future stars if these two are nurtured well and utilised in a proper manner. If India has one gem in Kohli, the Lankans have two.

Inspite of the unwelcome loss to India in the all-important match, the Lankans fought on bravely against the Aussies in their last match of the league phase, a do or die one. Even though their strike bowler Malinga was mauled by the Indians and Kohli in particular, Jayawardene's continued faith in Malinga and the way he backed him ensured it was the same bowler who broke the Aussie's back in their not too challenging run chase which ensured the Lankans deservedly led the points table and entered the finals. As they say, fortune favours the brave and it is no surprise the Lankans have won 4 of their last 5 ODI's against the giant Aussies.

With the Asia Cup round the corner, the three sub-continent giants and Bangladesh are gearing up to play with aggression and win it. If the Lankans entered the CB Series completely down, it is now the Indian and Pakistan teams respectively, recently battered and bruised, who will be looking for a turnaround. If India has nothing to boast of after their performance down under nosedived, Pakistan, though began their Test series with England with a bang, subsequently succumbed to their rivals in both the shorter versions of the game. But Pakistan is renowned for always coming up with a surprise element and their never say die attitude will keep them in the reckoning throughout the tournament. Though it is expected that two teams amongst India, Pakistan and Sri Lanka will make it to the finals, Bangladesh too will fancy their chances as they are playing at home and are well known for pulling the carpet from under the big guns' feet. One morale booster for the teams playing in the Asia Cup is the typical sub-continent condition. In the sub-continent, these teams are always tigers. At the end, only one will emerge a tiger and the rest, paper tigers.

The ODI's and T20's between the Proteas and the Kiwis certainly did not live up to the expectations of throwing up a stiff fight. New Zealand's fate was similar to that of Pakistan in the similar versions against England. The home advantage held by the Kiwis went abegging as both their batsmen and bowlers did not live up to their expectations. Ofcourse, full credit goes to the South Africans for their dominating display throughout. The Test series has begun and let us hope the Kiwis turn it around atleast now. So far, the Kiwi bowling appears to be back in it's groove when they tested and prevailed over the Proteas in the first innings of the first Test. It was a treat to watch the rhythm of Chris Martin. Hope the good work continues to make the series an interesting one.

The Aussies will leave for the Caribbean within days after lifting the CB Series cup to take part in a series against the West Indies comprising of 5 ODI's, 2 T20's and 3 Tests. An absorbing contest is due, though the continued exclusion of Chris Gayle from the team is disappointing. It is very sad for international cricket and the West Indies in particular, as their cricketer Runako Morton died in a recent car crash. An ODI specialist, Morton has played in 15 Tests, 56 ODI's and a lone T20 for his country. He had scored two ODI 100's and a scintillating match-winning 90 n.o against the Aussies in the 2006 Champions Trophy. Let's hope the Windies emerge winners and dedicate their win to Runako Morton.

CHAPTER FORTY-FIVE

LONG BATTLE AHEAD FOR SHORTEST FORMAT

(Week ending September 15, 2012)

It is now the T20 season again. The 2012 T20 world cup in Sri Lanka is just a few days away and teams are already busy playing warm up matches. For the first time, it looks like the minnows are going to give the big men a run for their money. This is thanks to their current fine form coupled with increase in confidence levels and also due to the unpredictable nature of this format. In other words, one can say there are no minnows in this edition or format. The peculiarity of T20 cricket is such that it will be foolish to predict a champion till the last match is played or the last ball is bowled.

The teams are divided into 4 groups with 3 in each group and the top two from each group will qualify for the next stage. Ireland and Afghanistan have come here through the qualifiers' grind and they thoroughly deserve to be here. Ireland are in high spirits, especially after having overtaken the Aussies briefly in the T20 rankings recently. On paper, Group D comprising of Pakistan, New Zealand and Bangladesh appears to be the group of death with Group C which includes Sri Lanka, South Africa and Zimbabwe not lagging much behind.

Group B can turn out the group of upsets as Ireland are in fine form and the Aussies and the West Indies are currently the most vulnerable in this format. Though Group A should not pose any problems to India and England, the clash between them is expected to be a cracker and probably one of the biggest matches of the competition. In the second round of 8 teams, each team will play one opponent each from the other three groups respectively. The top four from this group will make it to the semi-finals.

Some of the teams are already warmed up going into the world cup, thanks to the recent T20 series played between Pakistan vs. Australia, England vs South Africa and India vs. New Zealand. Each of these produced different results, clearly reconfirming the uncertainities involved in the shortest format. While England drew 1-1 with South Africa, Pakistan failed to clean sweep their series against the Kangaroos, winning 2-1. The Kiwis who succumbed in the Test series without a fight brought out their best in the lone T20 match played against India in Chennai. This means India, the first T20 world cup winners in 2007 are yet to beat the Kiwis in a T20 match and Indian fans will have to wait for another day for their team to overcome this jinx.

Inspite of being in a very comfortable position to achieve the target till their skipper Dhoni stepped in, India faltered in the last couple of overs. Losing a T20 match by a run inspite of having 6 wickets in hand does not reflect a confident batting line-up. The earlier India overcome this deficiency, it is better for them, especially with the world cup round the corner. The only consolation for the hosts is the emotional and confident return of Yuvraj Singh who did reasonably well to take a catch and hit some lusty blows.

The tough will get going when the going gets tough, but only the shrewdest will win the cup!

CHAPTER FORTY-SIX

MOST STARS YET TO MAKE A MARK

(Week ending April 21, 2012)

With almost one third of the matches having been played, the IPL 5 is getting hotter by the day. Just like the other editions, this one too is seeing heroes and zeros. Indian batsman Ajinjkya Rahane has been the find with the bat. The only centurion in this IPL, his 318 from 5 matches is far ahead from the rest of the pack with no one even near the 200 mark yet. It is not just the runs that speak high of Rahane, but the ease and confidence with which he bats. He is also the most technically sound amongst the current lot of aspiring youngsters. With some of the senior Indian batsmen set to retire in the near future closely following Rahul Dravid, Rahane's class, consistency and strike rate come in as perfect replacements in all the formats of the game for Team India.

Having made his first class debut in 2007, he has represented India in 11 ODI's and 2 T20's till date. But the irony is, it is the IPL which has brought him to limelight with everyone bowing to his game now and there are sure signs of him making it big in international cricket very soon. His first first class outing saw him make 143 and in his first 50 matches, he went on to score 4,862 runs with 18 centuries and 18 fifties. Having scored a 98, he followed it with a 100, first in this IPL. As if this is not enough, he hit 6 fours in an over, the first ever in T20 cricket. His debut international for India in the T20 against England saw him maul the English attack for a 38 ball 61 only to be dropped soon after.

In the bowling front, it is Shahbaz Nadeem of Delhi who is running away with honours. The initial matches saw Kevon Cooper shine for Rajasthan. But now, the bowling hero seems to be Nadeem. He hasn't got a big haul yet, but the big wickets and his stunning economy rate have been his hallmark. He is aged 23 and has played only a meagre 24 T20 games thus far. Hailing from Jharkhand, the slow and lean left arm spinner has his skipper Sehwag's confidence and immense trust on him and this backing has helped him excel. He has played in all five of Delhi's matches so far and has figures of 2 for 14 (Mumbai), 3 for 16 (Deccan Chargers), 0 for 9 (Chennai), 0 for 16 (KKR) and 1 for 26 (RCB). This performance is not only stupendous, but also unbelievable as these are from T20, the IPL, where huge scores are the order of the day. His prize scalps included batsmen like Richard Levi, Devy Jacobs, Duminy, Shikhar Dhawan and Parthiv Patel.

On the other hand, there are some big names in batting who are yet to click. They are rather a disappointment. Some of them are Brendon McCullum, Virat Kohli, Ross Taylor, Virender Sehwag, Richard Levi, Murali Vijay, Yusuf Pathan and Suresh Raina. Let us hope as the tourney progresses, these big guns step in with vital knocks and salvage their respective pride. It's a similar story with leading bowlers as well with Morne Morkel and Munaf Patel being the only exceptions.

The West Indies are at their favourite game yet again. Not cricket, but their love for throwing away positions of comfort or dominance. If they had lost the first Test from nowhere, they blew away the chance of dominating the second. For them, it is becoming a case of old wine in a new bottle with every match being played. Having lost the first Test, the second Test was a must win for them to level the series. First, they allowed the Aussies to put up an unexpected total of over 300 mainly with the help of their ever reliable Mike Hussey supported by the tailenders. While batting, inspite of some initial hiccups, the Windies recovered fantastically through Chanderpaul and Bravo and were set to overtake the Aussies' total and gain a substantial lead being placed at 230 for 4. The Kangaroos were themselves surprised to see the Windies collapse like a pack of cards and lose 5 wicket for just 19 runs, all to Nathan Lyon, the harmless spinner. Eventually, they folded for 257.

With the weather playing spoil sport on each of the first four days, a result now looks highly unlikely and the Aussies are set to walk away with a 1-0 series win unless the Windies do another hara-kiri on the last day to make it 2-0 in favour of Australia.

In a sad development, Bangladesh's impending tour of Pakistan has been deferred by a court order in response to a petition citing insecurity. Like cricket matches, cricket tours are also of glorious uncertainities!

CHAPTER FORTY-SEVEN

NEW ASPIRATIONS MARK NEW YEAR

(Week ending January 12, 2013)

Australia are set to play Sri Lanka in an ODI series after drubbing them in the just concluded Test series 3-0 while India are back against England in a 5 match ODI series after getting thoroughly drubbed by England in the Test series and Pakistan in the just concluded ODI series respectively. Both India and Australia were lacking in confidence a month ago. It is to Australia's credit they addressed all the issues on hand to gain their confidence back whilst India's confidence slid down further. The teams' respective approach was clearly visible from the transformation in results. Whilst Australia believed in themselves and came back with a positive attitude, India either failed to identify the causes for the repeated failures or failed to implement remedial measures for causes identified.

In addition to losing the Test series, Sri Lanka has been unfortunate to lose some key players including Kumara Sangakkara, their batting mainstay to injuries, leaving them out of the ODI series. Though the man in form Lasith Malinga is set to return, it is unlikely Sri Lanka's fortunes will change as they will struggle against the Aussie quickies. Malinga and players like Angelo Mathews may excel in patches, but most likely fail to achieve the desired consistency required to edge out the hosts in the 5 match series.

India, who are yet to get back to winning ways are still reeling under the shock 1-2 home defeat to arch rivals Pakistan in the 3 match ODI series. Their cup of woes continued with their top batsmen continuing to disappoint. The series could have well seen Pakistan whitewash India but for India's miraculous escape from the jaws of defeat defending a paltry score in the 3rd ODI. Pakistan let go a golden opportunity to clean sweep the series but atleast returned with the satisfaction of having inflicted a home ODI series defeat on India, the last one being five years ago. Bhuvaneshwar Kumar, Shami Ahmed and Dhoni's return to form have been the only gains for India from the series.

For India, the ongoing ODI series against England is the best chance to revive their dwindling fortunes. With the series set to be played on dull and placid wickets, India's batsmen are expected to regain their lost touch and present their fans with a long awaited series win and end India's winless drought. India has taken a big risk by keeping out their star Virender Sehwag, making him the scapegoat for all the recent previous defeats. Looking into the available options, Sehwag's replacement Pujara may cool his heels on the benches making his selection a meaningless exercise. By persisting with the other failing batsmen, the selectors have given them a chance yet again to either perform or expose themselves further.

Having lost the first Test to hosts South Africa by an innings, the Kiwis will go all out to win the ongoing second and final Test to level the series. Unfit Vernon Philander who wrecked and demolished the visitors for 45 in the first Test is out of this Test which should be a relief for New Zealand. However, change of the skipper just before the series seems to have not changed Kiwi's fortunes.

Barring South Africa, most teams will aspire to change their fortunes in 2013!

CHAPTER FORTY-EIGHT

A PASSIONATE GENIUS WHOM RECORDS CHASED

(Week ending November 16, 2013)

Though the game of cricket witnessed many an event between November 1989 and November 2013 with many players beginning and ending their respective international careers, a short little master stood tall and was busy mesmerizing the world of cricket. He is the only cricketer to have spanned over three generations of international cricketers. Sachin Ramesh Tendulkar started playing for India at 16 when every other schoolboy in India was tensed up preparing for his exams. It wasn't surely an age to face a battery of international pace bowlers but Sachin surely had other ideas and emerged the most respected cricketer of his era.

Nearing 16,000 Test runs, scoring the first double in ODI's and achieving the landmark hundredth century came towards the fag end of his career, but the path he tread was strewn with roses known as records. What has he not achieved in international cricket? Perhaps it is easier to make a list of his non-achievements and surely it will be a very short one. Inspite of being the only batsman to have scored most in three world cups, an ODI world cup evaded him for quite a while but knowing his passion and dedication very well, it was only a matter of time before he added this feather too to his cap in 2011. Just like his runs, the number of Tests and ODI's he has played for India speak volumes of his longevity. One has never seen a glimpse of tiredness or fatigue in this legend throughout his career and the fact that he has fought many an injury and niggle reaffirms his passion and dedication for the game.

His records are there to speak for him and yes, they are very special as they were always coming whenever he stepped on the field. It is said records are to be broken and it is possible very few of his stupendous achievements may be surpassed in the years or decades to come. But what will remain in the hearts of millions of cricket admirers is the special way and the consistency with which this little genius approached the game, match after match. What will remain etched in everyone's memory and can never be matched are his elegance, passion, commitment, dedication and the list can go on and on. The cricketing world and India in particular, will in the next few days, start missing on the field, the legend who often brought the nation to a grinding halt and filled millions of hearts with immeasurable self-esteem. We will never be able to see live the impeccable straight drives, precise cover drives, the famous flick down the leg side or the ever perfect paddle sweep from the master's blade henceforth.

He has already pumped in immense joy and pride in every Indian's heart that it will last a lifetime and till another genius will step in, probably only as a substitute. He is set to wield his willow for one last time this week. He is sure to exit with yet another magical touch. May be, he will get a century or not, but his knocks over the years will be replayed in every cricket fan's mind and heart for many years to come. The last few days have seen everything said about him by each and every cricketing expert including former greats and still the praise goes on. All eyes will be on Wankhede Stadium to witness the Master's swan song, may be yet another special one. If cricket is a religion in India today, it's because of this man.

His biggest plus point has been his on-field as well as off-field conduct. Whenever he stepped out to bat, we expected centuries to come and how can we forget him for centuries to come? What will happen to his fans after he exits? But the bigger question is, how will Sachin himself handle his retirement after loving and living cricket for over two decades?

CHAPTER FORTY-NINE

NO ROOM FOR THE IPL WINDOW

(Week ending June 16, 2012)

Pakistan began their ODI series against Sri Lanka after dominating most of their recent head to head clashes. This is mainly due to their accurate and balanced bowling attack. The presence of two spin-bowling all-rounders has given their team the affordability of trying various team compositions.

Though their bowlers have been helping the team's cause, the batsmen are yet to rise to the occasion. On the other hand, Sri Lankan senior batsmen too are finding it rather tough to make significant contributions to their team. This has exposed the relatively young and inexperienced middle order batsmen. But the Lankans were quick to adjust and succeed in their experimentation in the second match when their batsmen successfully posted a huge total. The Lankans have a right mix of youth and experience in their batting. It is a matter of time before they find the right combination as well as batting order which will certainly boost their chances in the future outings. The earlier they do it, it is better for them.

On the other hand, Pakistan opted to play only five specialist batsmen in their first two matches. Though they managed to win the first game with ease as they were chasing a modest total of 136, their batting was thoroughly exposed in the second when they succumbed to pressure in pursuit of 281. May be, they are playing a batsman short, a slot they are sacrificing or foregoing by opting to rely more on their bowlers. The third match was no different to them. Fortune favoured them by way of rain when the match was abandoned after the initial few overs with Pakistan reeling at 12 for 2 off 6 overs. They need to do a balancing act in their team selection for the remaining two matches if they want to win this ODI series.

Chris Gayle finally made a return to the West Indies team in their tour match against Middlesex. Though he made only 34 in this match, he made a mark in the bowling by claiming 2 for 0. But the story is set to be different when the ODI series begins. England will surely be well aware of this and must be spending most of their time strategizing ways to tackle the oncoming Gayle storm.

In a latest development, the ICC has decided against creating a separate window for the IPL. This is with a view to ensuring no precedent is set. Right from the inception of the IPL in 2008, schedules have clashed often. This has led to either players skipping national duties or players from teams like England finding themselves not in a position to play the IPL as their team is always busy during this time of the year. The coming IPL season will see New Zealand visiting England during the same time. Time will tell whether most of the Kiwi players will opt to play IPL and mint money or put on national caps.

The ICC fears including IPL in the future tour programmes will force them to accommodate other countries with similar leagues. Too much of the shortest form of cricket, especially by clubs in leagues will kill spectator interest and diminish the charm of international cricket.

ICC, please preserve Test cricket. Do not test cricket1

CHAPTER FIFTY

OPTIMISTIC INDIA BOUNCE BACK

(Week ending January 19, 2013)

The current ODI series between India and England has seen contrasting performances so far. With the third match set to be played today, the series is level at 1-1. While England won the first at Rajkot, India bounced back in style to trounce the visitors in the Kochi match. The Rajkot win for England came after two successive ODI series defeats of 0-5 in Indian soil for them. This win turned out to be only the second in their last 13 encounters against India in India. This surely was a much awaited moment, raising hopes and expectations of a repeat of the recent Test performances. But the second ODI saw the Indians come to their groove under tailor-made home conditions including the vociferous crowd support.

If Monty Panesar scripted an England Test series win earlier, it was Samit Patel who bludgeoned the Indian bowling in the first ODI. Both players are interestingly of Indian origin. Patel's heroics in the last two overs cost India the match. Inspite of chasing a mammoth total of 325, India managed to come very close only to lose by 9 runs. For the first time, the four top order batsmen managed to put up decent scores to bring their team closer to victory. But it turned out insufficient as once the Raina-Dhoni partnership was broken, the scales tilted in favour of England.

The last ODI against Pakistan saw debutant Shami Ahmed bowl excellently including a record four consecutive maidens on debut for India. Indian skipper Dhoni erred yet again in leaving out Shami Ahmed at Kochi which proved quite expensive. The Indian bowlers looked toothless in Rajkot allowing England to run away with a dream total. India boasts of it's spinners but it was man of the match English spinner Tredwell who had the last laugh with a brilliant 4 for 44. Though the recent emergence of Bhuvaneshwar Kumar and Shami Ahmed are positive signs, the earlier India sorts out their bowling woes, it is better for them.

The second match saw the usual collapse of the top batsmen which has now become a routine. But the stunning batting display of Suresh Raina, Dhoni and Ravindra Jadeja in the latter stages of the innings took the game away from England. Though Dhoni was the top scorer yet again, it was Jadeja who turned the tables in India's favour. It appears he has finally justified his inclusion as an all-rounder. It was clean hitting throughout, followed by a couple of wickets and a brilliant run out which ultimately gave him the man of the match award. From here on, it looks like India are favourites as they seem to have found the winning ways atlast.

The Proteas won the Test series 2-0 as expected against the Kiwis who had no answers to the hosts' pace battery. The only glimmer of hope for them now is the oncoming ODI series but it looks highly unlikely if they can produce different results. It appears the problems are more to do with temperament for New Zealand rather than form or class.

Down under, the Lankans have produced their first win on this tour by winning the second ODI to level the series 1-1. Probably the Lankans have a plan up their sleeve and will produce a surprising result.

CHAPTER FIFTY-ONE

PETERSEN AND PIETERSEN DOMINATE

(Week ending August 11, 2012)

What looked so near to South Africa after the 1st Test win is still a distance away. With the 2nd Test drawn, the final Test is set to be a thrilling encounter and hopefully, will produce a nailbiting finish. For England, it is a must win match, whereas for the Proteas, a draw will do the trick and the Test supremacy will dawn on them.

The drawn second Test turned out into a see-saw battle with honours shared evenly at the end. The first innings of both sides saw batsmen from either side dominating whilst the second innings for them were dominated by bowlers. With weather playing spoil sport on and off, the match saw two centurions, one from either side with each side managing a little over 400 in the first innings respectively. For the Proteas, Petersen produced a brilliant 182 inspite of their prominent batsmen failing and it was Pietersen's cameo of 149 runs which helped England in the first innings. The English skipper is yet to make a noteworthy contribution in this series and if this extends to the third Test, it is bound to dent England's chances of retaining the no.1 slot.

In the Caribbean, West Indies created history when they beat New Zealand 2-0 to win the series and register two successive Test wins after more than a decade. This visit by the Kiwis must have given the hosts their best bounty of wins ever as they won 2-0 in the T20's, 4-1 in the ODI's and 2-0 in the Tests. Though the presence of Gayle and Sunil Narinc did wonders, West Indies' star in the third Test was Marlon Samuels with brilliant knocks of 123 and 52.

The result of the lone T20 played between India and Sri Lanka following the ODI series was no different and gave the Indians yet another well deserved win. The match saw the Lankans put India in to bat and inspite of the usual blitzkreig from their in form batsman Virat Kohli, India squandered yet another good start to end their innings well below the expected total. Fortunately for India, they were brought back into the game by their bowlers. Pathan with 3 wickets utilized his lucky inclusion to cement his place in the team atleast for the coming months and Ashok Dinda had a dream spell claiming 4 wickets, 3 of them coming in one over. This win should keep India in good spirits going into the T20 world cup to be held shortly in Sri Lanka.

Within a few days after their returning home, India is set to take on New Zealand in a two Test series. The Kiwis' confidence is not expected to be high after their recent drubbing in the hands of the West Indies coupled with the absence of their prime spinner Daniel Vettori owing to a groin injury. On the other hand, India will be looking to regain some of the pride they lost in the hands of England and Australia in the recent months. It will be interesting to see India playing a Test series sans their wall Rahul Dravid, their anchor man in the last couple of decades. His retirement has certainly created a void in the Indian batting line-up which will be extremely difficult to fill.

CHAPTER FIFTY-TWO

PROTEAS, AMLA AND SMITH CREATE HISTORY

(Week ending July 28, 2012)

When England finished the first day of the first Test at 267 for 3, they would not have dreamt they will receive a jolt in the coming days. In fact, England dominated the Test only on day one and the rest of the days belonged to South Africa as England were cornered, only to watch the proceedings helplessly. First, it was Dale Steyn who came into his groove early on in the second day to brighten things for the visitors. England losing 4 quick wickets early in the second day was undoubtedly the turning point of the match.

The incredible innings played by Hashim Amla to remain unbeaten on 311 will be written in Proteas' cricketing history in golden letters. This enabled his team to register the first ever Test victory at the Oval. This win came in the 14th outing here with 7 wins for England, 6 drawn and this historic win for South Africa. The margin in victories on this ground clearly shows how dominant England were over the years and what an unphill task it was for the Proteas, especially after having nothing to smile about on day one.

South Africa are now close to becoming the no.1 Test team. With two Tests remaining, the battering received by England has now clearly made Smith's men the favourites in the series. In the process, Amla became the highest run scorer in a Test innings for his country, reached his as well as his country's first triple hundred and remained unconquered in the process just like in his previous best score of 253 n.o. against India. This goes to prove what a determined character he is. Inspite of losing his opening partner early, Graeme Smith went on to compile a hundred as well alongwith Jacques Kallis who too scored only his second Test hundred in England.

Smith's 100 came in his 100th Test and he became only the 7th international cricketer to achieve this feat. Smith has currently flown home to welcome his new born daughter and will return in time for the second Test. With Dale Steyn striking form in the second innings, Smith will be restless to wrest the throne from England with a series win knowing very well it was his team who gave England their previous home series loss four years ago.

West Indies are delighted with Chris Gayle's return to their Test squad against the Kiwis after a gap of 18 months. His presence, alongwith that of Sunil Naraine will surely give the hosts a big edge. Ever since Gayle was kept out of the team, the Windies' makeshift openers have managed only 3 half century partnerships in 31 innings and their average partnership this year against the Aussies is only 14.45. This clearly shows why Gayle's presence is a must. With players like Roach, Chanderpaul and Deo Naraine too returning to the squad, the hosts will have a huge advantage, especially with Sunil Naraine bowling on the spin friendly tracks.

In Sri Lanka, having lost the first ODI, the hosts skittled India for their second lowest total in the island and registered a thumping win to level the series 1-1. With 3 matches remaining, the series now looks evenly poised and will prove a litmus test to the world champions.

CHAPTER FIFTY-THREE

RARE INDIAN HAT-TRICK ON LANKAN SOIL

(Week ending August 04, 2012)

It was a proud moment for Indian cricket when they achieved their 400th victory in ODI's by beating Sri Lanka in the 4th match of the current series. This match was the 3,294th official ODI and more than 10% of the wins have been registered by India. This goes on to show the huge number of matches India has played since inception of this format.

This win also enabled the Indians to gain an unassailable 3-1 lead in the 5 match series. Batting first in the first two matches gave the Indians mixed results. Their batsmen were on a roll in the first one, only to put up a dismal show to lose the second one. The wins in the last two matches reconfirmed India's consistent success while chasing. This is India's 3rd bilateral series win in Sri Lanka in the last 4 years though it took them 23 years to achieve the first one in 2008.

The star of not only this series, but of the last few years for India has been their rising star Virat Kohli. He has already conquered unimaginable heights in international cricket and a special place in the hearts of the Indian as well as cricket fans in general. His achievements speak volumes for him. But for a rare one off failure, he is always there for his team. He reached his 13th ODI hundred in this match from only 86 innings, a record previously held by Proteas' A B De Villiers who did it in 121 innings. This gap clearly shows the consistent scoring pattern of the young Kohli.

He has already scored over 800 runs in his last ten ODI innings. Scoring over a 1,000 runs in a calendar year used to be an uphill task a few years ago. Kohli has proudly surpassed the 1,000 mark for 2012 with ease, a repeat of 2011 . His last 8 innings include 5 centuries. A batsman who never panics, Kohli has always handled almost every international bowler with disdain and ease. For aspiring and budding youngsters, Kohli is certainly a live manual to watch and follow.

Back in England, the ongoing second Test can turn into a dream come true for South Africa if they play with the same attitude and confidence as in the first. The opening partnership of 120 on day one should give the Proteas the much needed confidence to wrap up the series as well as grab the top slot. England, who have held on to the no.1 slot with lots of grit will throw everything and will leave no stone unturned to stop the Proteas' march. The only worrying factor will be the no.6 slot yet again. With Bopara withdrawing citing personal reasons, his replacement Taylor will be expected to grab the opportunity with both hands and justify his unexpected inclusion.

It is now 10 years since the West Indies have won two Tests consecutively. Having won the first Test against the Kiwis, can they do it now in the second and final Test? New Zealand have lost all but one outing in this series so far. Can they rewrite the script and level the series? It can turn out their best gift to their coach John Wright in his final assignment.

CHAPTER FIFTY-FOUR

RIGID INDIA'S MISERY CONTINUES

(Week ending December 29, 2012)

South Africa reaffirmed their T20 supremacy over New Zealand by winning the 3rd match to make it a 2-1 series victory. After winning the first match, the hosts allowed the Kiwis to fight back and win the second. This win was mainly due to a magnificient hundred by Martin Guptill which enabled his team to chase the target and clinch a last ball thriller. The last ball boundary not only ensured New Zealand levelled the series but also enabled Guptill reach his well deserved century.

In this series, Richard Levi failed to live upto his expectations while Henry Davids chipped in with two very useful half centuries during the series with the final one ensuring his team wrapped up the series. South Africa's total of 179 for 6 is the fifth highest international as well as domestic total in this format at this ground. Though the Kiwis gave an impression of repeating the heroics of the second match till the 11th over, the latter stages saw their batsmen crumbling under pressure to the bowling of Aaron Phangiso and Ryan McLaren. Phangiso who was struggling in the previous match as a debutant and Ryan McLaren grabbed 3 wickets apiece at a crucial stage to tighten the noose around the Kiwis' neck.

Australia are ready to give Sri Lanka a knock-out punch in the Boxing Day Test. Put in to bat, Sri Lanka could muster only 156, mainly due to Sangakkara's resistance which also enabled him enter the history books by crossing 10,000 Test runs. Centurion Michael Clarke has now scored most Test runs in a calendar year for Australia.

India's misery continued with a loss to neighbours Pakistan in the first T20 match. Many factors can be attributed to India's continuous and consistent dismal shows. A few of them are poor team selection, over dependence on batsmen, strange batting order, increasing off-field concerns, lack of efforts on the field, absence of killer instinct, poor on-field tactics, etc., Put in to bat, India made hara-kiri of a dream start by the openers. At one stage, they looked like ending up near the 200 mark, only to struggle to reach a pathetic 133, thanks to the last 8 wickets falling for around 50 runs.

India played 8 batsmen with Ashwin, a genuine spinner, sitting out. India was blessed to have Bhuvaneshwar Kumar, the debutant, in the squad. His figures of 3 for 9 won many a heart and rattled many a Pakistani batsman. The visitors who were reeling at 12 for 3 were let off the hook, thanks to Dhoni's audacity to bring in part timer Virat Kohli at a critical juncture enabling Pakistan to pile up some vital runs. The match also saw the customary flaring up of tempers.

With 11 runs needed, Dhoni surprisingly gave the last over to off-colour Ravindra Jadeja who expectedly gave away the match, much to the dismay of Indian supporters. India will now play the remaining T20 on Friday at Ahmedabad. Nothing has worked for India in this year and the skipper and his team must be waiting to bid farewell to 2012 and welcome the new year with a ray of hope.

One thing is certain, the new year will change either India's fortunes or it's captain!

CHAPTER FIFTY-FIVE

SHORTEST FORMAT, LONGEST ENTERTAINMENT

(Week ending April 07, 2012)

The IPL 5 has begun. The opening ceremony was in typical Bollywood style, the only exception being it had a Hollywood touch as well. Exactly after a year since India won the last world cup played in the sub-continent, the IPL kicked off on April 4, 2012 with the first match seeing the holders Chennai Super Kings lose to the Champions League winner, Mumbai Indians. The second match saw Delhi Dare Devils almost making a mess of the wonderful start given by their ace bowler Morne Morkel. In a rain affected match of 12 overs, Delhi successfully restricted Kolkata Knight Riders to 97 only to almost falter in their chase before Irfan Pathan clinched the game with an unbeaten hurricane 42. The current edition of the IPL will surely act as the much needed remedy to heal the Indian fans' wounds sustained in the last one year following the world cup triumph.

The matches, 76 in total, promise a grand feast to cricket fans world over. The opening ceremony saw leading Bollywood icons like Amitabh Bachchan, Kareena Kapoor, Priyanka Chopra, Salman Khan, the Colonial Cousins and Prabhudeva entertain the crowd. The icing on the cake was Katty Perry's appearance and performance at the end which was purely top-class. In between, the captains of all the teams joined together to sign the pledge to play the game in the right spirit, with integrity and dignity.

The last few months saw Indian cricket at it's lowest ebb, losing 8 overseas Tests on the trot, 4 each to England and Australia respectively. If Dhoni's captaincy in the last few years saw everything he touched turn into gold, the last few months in contrast saw him groping for confidence in leadership, especially in the Test format, after seeing his team battered and bruised in the longer version. May be, the IPL will give Team India the required confidence before they take on Australia, England and South Africa respectively at home later in the year.

The one-off T20 between India and South Africa played recently ended in no result due to rain interruption after what was turning out into a keenly fought contest. Though the Proteas butchered the Indian attack to reach 220, India replied strongly with an unbroken opening stand, raising hopes of yet another successful historic chase, before rain played spoilsport. It is a pity such short format one-off matches are organised during the rainy season. India travelled a long way to play this T20 match, the duration of which is not even 1/3rd of their one way flight from Mumbai to Johannesburg.

With the ODI series and T20 series tied at 2-2 and 1-1 respectively, Australia and West Indies will begin their 3 Test series today. A win in this series will help the Aussies climb a notch up in the ICC rankings while for the West Indies, it will be just pride emanating from a historic series win. Looking at the recent see-saw battles between these two, the series is bound to go to the wire. Aussies might be overflowing with confidence after their recent crushing of India, but the Windies will always remain a tough nut to crack, especially at home.

Having lost the first Test to Sri Lanka, a repeat of their recent performance against Pakistan, England had their backs to the wall going into the 2nd Test. Failure to win this match meant surrendering the no.1 Test ranking to South Africa. Having been at the receiving end, Strauss and his men rose to the occasion in style to show yet again why they are a top Test side. Strong contributions by most of their top batsmen and a century by Kevin Pietersen ensured they gained a sizeable first innings lead of 185 to be well placed at the end of the third day and they now look certain to win this Test and save their face as well as their top spot, atleast for the time being. However, South Africa who have been breathing down their neck are bound to continue doing so.

With the leading Australian cricketers set to join the IPL at a later stage, the league is bound to get tougher in the days to come. Played on batsmen friendly wickets and with explosive openers like David Warner, Sehwag, Finch, Brendon Mcullum, Chris Gayle and the new South African sensation Richard Levi around, most of the teams will look forward to rollicking starts and this edition will see many high scoring matches. One thing is for sure, the bowlers will be made to toil hard. This is the time when cricket elsewhere in the world comes to a grinding halt and the streets in India wear a deserted look in the evenings. The format is shortest, but the entertainment, non-stop and longest!

CHAPTER FIFTY-SIX

SIMILAR TEAMS IN FAMILIAR CONDITIONS

(Week ending March 17, 2012)

The Asia Cup which began in the sub-continent on Sunday saw similar teams playing in familiar conditions. While Pakistan who almost lost to Bangladesh in the opening match pulled things back at the last moment to snatch a 21 run win, India steamrolled into a convincing win over Sri Lanka by putting up a mammoth score of over 300 to win by 50 runs. With India winning over Sri Lanka, the match between Pakistan and Sri Lanka is bound to become very interesting and gains more significance as each of these two teams would like to win it to take a step closer to the finals. Pakistan's win over Bangladesh is their 29th win out of 30 encounters between them. Though they continued their dominance, this win is certainly not one of their best as the match saw their batsmen make a mockery of their brilliant opening stand of over 100 and only a late cameo by Umar Gul ensured they went past the 250 mark. The Pakistan batsmen need to quickly come into their groove in the remaining matches as they will be facing much tougher opponents and the path to the finals will not be a rosy one.

On the other hand, though Tendulkar failed yet again in the first match to achieve the landmark 100, the men in form, Gambhir and Kohli continued with their stellar performances. Their double century partnership, India's 7th against the Sri Lankans and 19th overall in ODI's resulted in both of them making well deserved 100's. In the process, Virat Kohli's century made him the quickest to reach 10 ODI hundreds in just 83 matches, bettering Gordon Greenidge's achievement in 99 matches. With this achievement, Virat Kohli has climbed a notch higher in international cricket. In comparison, recent greats like Brian Lara(109), Sachin Tendulkar(134) and Ricky Ponting(150) took more matches to achieve this feat. With this win, India has won 4 out of their last 5 matches against the Lankans, a feat similar to that of the Lankans over the Aussies in the recently concluded CB Series before losing the third final to the Aussies.

Sri Lanka will find it tough making it to the finals as injuries to their key players Thusara Periera and Angelo Mathews have kept them out of the Asia Cup. Mathews will be replaced by Shaminda Eranga and it will interesting to see if he can fill the void. In contrast to the recent ODI's played outside the subcontinent, the Asia Cup is bound to witness huge scores making even a target of over 300 unsafe.

The first Test between the Kiwis and Proteas which saw thrilling contests in the first four days ended in a disappointing draw. The fifth day was set up nicely with South Africa holding a slight edge considering the Kiwis were set a huge target going into the fifth day. However, rain played spoilsport to thwart the chances of any result. The return of Mark Gillespie in the New Zealand squad will boost their chances to turn it around in the Test series after giving away the T20 and ODI series on a platter respectively. South Africa went into the Test series with a chance to becoming the No.1 Test team by the end of this series. They needed a 3-0 clean sweep of the series to ensure this. With no result in the first Test, England will continue to be the No.1 Test team for some more time inspite of their pathetic 0-3 loss to Pakistan in their recent series.

Australia have embarked on their tour of the West Indies. Thanks to his comeback performance against India in the Test series, Ricky Ponting has been included in the Test squad inspite of being dropped from the ODI squad. Peter Forrest, rewarded for his debut ODI series performance and the left-arm spinner Michael Beer will join the Test squad while Shaun Marsh will sit out due to his recent dismal performances. A big treat is in store as the tour will consist of 5 ODI's, 2 T20's and 3 Tests as the Windies will be a tough nut to crack in their backyard.

Tuesday saw the beginning of the 12 day world T20 qualifier tournament in the UAE with 16 teams vying for the two top slots. With two teams set to make it to the main event, they are bound to engage in gruelling contests. The teams are split into two groups and the top three from each group will qualify for the knockout phase. The group winners face off in the first qualifying final after which the winner will qualify. The loser will join the other three to begin a fresh knock out phase for the remaining spot. Let's wait and see who joins the big guns in Sri Lanka in September!

CHAPTER FIFTY-SEVEN

SRI LANKA OUTSMART PAKISTAN

(Week ending June 23, 2012)

Kevin Pietersen's recent decision to retire from the shorter versions of the game is now followed by Shahid Afridi's talks of quitting ODI's and playing only T20 cricket for Pakistan. No wonder, this has raised many an eyebrow and has left everyone wondering as to what is happening behind the scenes in the Pakistan camp. Afridi feels he is not contributing much and also wants the youngsters to get a chance.

However, cricket experts are attributing this to either Afridi not being comfortable with the present set-up ever since he was removed as Pakistan captain sometime ago or is not happy with Mohammed Hafeez being made captain of the T20 team. With their coach Dave Whatmore laying stress on youngsters, Afridi might have got the message that seniors will be phased out slowly sooner than later. If and when he quits, Pakistan will certainly miss his services, the most significant for the team in recent years.

Pakistan had a great opportunity to level the ODI series going into the fifth match. At one stage, Pakistan had Sri Lanka's back to the wall with the hosts tottering in their chase and the match was almost over in Pakistan's favour. But Angelo Matthews had other ideas to come up with a cameo to remain unbeaten on 80 to see his team through to win the series, all this with the help of the tail-enders.

The ODI series began with great hopes for Pakistan, but their brittle batting ensured the team lost to the hosts 1-3. Added to this, their captain Misbah has been suspended from the first Test, thanks to his team's slow over rate in the fifth ODI. Pakistan still has a chance to restore lost pride when they take on the hosts in the Test series and for this, they have to raise their morale.

Misbah's absence means Mohammed Hafeez will lead Pakistan for the first time in a Test series. Again, Pakistan go into the series as favourites, having won their last four Test series on the trot which included a 3-0 sweep of the no.1 ranked England. On the other hand, Sri Lanka has played seven Test series ever since their star Muttiah Muralitharan retired in 2010. Losing four and drawing three of them means they are yet to win a series since then. Having won the ODI series, this will be their best chance.

The ODI series between England and West Indies saw England take an unassailable 2-0 lead with a match remaining. Though Chris Gayle proved his class yet again, his controversial dismissal triggered a mid inning collapse with his team losing 4 wickets for 16 runs, a collapse from which they never recovered. With a lone T20 to be played, West Indies need to win the third ODI to gain the much needed confidence.

After a long time, Zimbabwe is currently hosting an international series, the triangular T20 with South Africa and Bangladesh being the other teams. With two matches remaining in the league phase, it has been a closely fought series thus far keeping the chances of all teams alive. The final is set to be played this Sunday. Zimbabwe deservedly looks like making it to the finals as they are the only team to have beaten both the opponents atleast once each.

CHAPTER FIFTY-EIGHT

STRONG WINDIES MISS RUED CHANCES

(Week ending February 09, 2013)

At the end of the 3rd ODI, the West Indies skipper Darren Sammy was seen ruing the chances missed by his team. According to him and rightly so, these chances were potential match winning moments. Barring the first ODI where the Windies were routed, thanks to a fine spell by Mitchell Starc, the West Indies had chances of going up 2-1 at the end of the 3rd ODI in the five match series. But unfortunately for them, having lost the series 0-3 already, the remaining two matches they will play are only of academic interest.

The first ODI was decided in the first couple of hours when Sammy's men folded for a paltry 70 runs. But in the second match, the hosts were reeling at 98 for 6 only to be allowed to wriggle out, thanks to George Bailey's magnificient and stylish century. The Aussies were in front from the word go in the 3rd ODI, aided by a fine century by Shane Watson who was delighted by his return to form. In both these chases, the West Indies saw a ray of hope by way of long partnerships by the Bravo brothers. However, the team crumbled under pressure at the end only to snatch defeat from the jaws of victory.

Kieron Pollard on whom both their chases depended, did nothing more than taking a couple of stunning catches at the rope. Similarly, Chris Gayle and Sunil Narine, the men who matter, failed to live up to the expectations. Undoubtedly, this is one of the best combinations the Windies have had in the recent past and it is unfortunate they are woefully out of form as a team. Chris Gayle for West Indies and George Bailey for Australia are likely to sit out owing to injury concerns for the remaining matches.

In the neighbouring New Zealand, England are set to play 3 T20's, 3 ODI's and 3 Tests against the Kiwis. Former Kiwis skipper Ross Taylor will be back in action after a self-imposed exile due to his axing as the skipper after the 1-1 draw against Sri Lanka recently. His absence in the recent tour of South Africa was felt heavily as the Kiwis lost the Test and the T20 series. Only a ODI series victory salvaged some pride for them. Taylor's axing first hurt him and then went on to hurt New Zealand cricket as the whole episode was thoroughly mishandled.

In South Africa, the Proteas beat Pakistan in the first Test convincingly inspite of their first innings folding on day one, a rarity. Dale Steyn left Pakistan dumbfounded with his double 5 wicket haul for the match. Clueless Pakistan were also skittled for a first innings score of 49, their lowest Test total ever. During the week, Hashim Amla became only the second cricketer after Ponting to lead Tests and ODI batting rankings simultaneously.

The women's world cup is currently being played in India. Sri Lanka has been the team of the tournament so far undoubtedly. For the first time in their history, they beat England as well as India respectively. Three teams, barring hosts India and Pakistan, qualified from each group to the super six, carrying forward the points earned in the group stage. The top two from here will play the finals!

CHAPTER FIFTY-NINE

STRUGGLING MINNOWS FAIL TO IMPRESS

(Week ending September 22, 2012)

The T20 world cup began on Tuesday with the hosts Sri Lanka playing Zimbabwe in the opening match. Though the warm up matches produced mixed results giving an impression that the minnows may come up with an upset or two, they failed to cash in on the uncertainities of the shortest format. Teams like Zimbabwe, Ireland and Afghanistan succumbed to the pressure of the big stage without putting up any resistance or semblance of a fight.

Sri Lanka, India, Australia and South Africa registered easy victories to start with as all these teams were untested and scrapped through, almost assured of a place in the second round. Unlike the 50 over format, the current edition of the T20 world cup does not offer a second chance to the teams who lose their first match except in groups where the three teams are equally balanced and the matches are expected to be close ones. Thus, the minnows failed to capitalize on the supposedly lone chance of making it to the second round.

It was Mendis' show for Sri Lanka with Jeevan Mendis shining with both bat and ball and Ajanta Mendis mesmerizing the Zimbabwe batsmen with a record 6 for 8. For the Aussies, it was the usual solitary show by Shane Watson both with the bat and the ball. For India, though Virat Kohli excelled with yet another fifty, especially after the openers surprisingly failed against the Afghan attack and the bowlers chipped in with timely spells, the Afghan fielders equally contributed to the Indian win by dropping as many as half a dozen catches allowing the Indians to get away. There were atleast a few moments when Afghanistan had an outside chance of upsetting India, but lack of self-belief, confidence and experience, especially of playing against big teams undid them.

The match between Ireland and Australia turned out to be a non contest with Ireland not living upto the expectations, especially after the recent ranking tussle. Zimbabwe have now lost both their matches. In their second match, Jacques Kallis' fiery spell of 4 for 15 demolished them and the Proteas surpassed the target without any loss with Richard Levi getting an unbeaten 50. They are oozing with confidence after their recent fine show at England and are certainly one of the favourites in this edition.

With Zimbabwe crashing out early, the Group C match between Sri Lanka and South Africa, though may produce some fireworks, will only be of academic interest as they both have already qualified for the next stage. The Group D matches which will be played at the end will attract lot of interest as this is the group of death. Bangladesh will be determined to prove a point and Pakistan and the Kiwis cannot afford to relax. Any momentary lapse from them will see them bid adieu to their aspirations of progressing further.

The second round will see the big teams involved in close encounters. India, Australia, South Africa and Pakistan or Bangladesh are set to fight it out in one group whilst England, Sri Lanka, West Indies and New Zealand or Bangladesh will form the other group.

Watch out for favourites West Indies. Though Chris Gayle feels right team balance is essential, they are always special, especially with their team combination!

CHAPTER SIXTY

T20 WORLD CUP AWAITS A NEW CHAMPION

(Week ending October 06, 2012)

The super eight stage of the T20 world cup saw the most deserving teams make it to the semi-finals. Australia, Pakistan, hosts Sri Lanka and the ever entertaining West Indies have remained on the top half of the super 8 to vie for the finals. Holder England's recent woes extended to this event when they failed to make it to the last four. India was not far behind. Having won the first T20 world cup in 2007, they are yet to qualify for semi-finals in this event since then and in fact, had never won a super eight match after their 2007 triumph and this jinx was broken in the current edition only.

The first semi-final saw Pakistan squander a very big advantage when they restricted Sri Lanka to only 139/4. Inspite of having a rollicking start, the Lankans faltered in the last 6 overs to set up a meagre target. However, shrewd captaincy and intelligent bowling changes by Mahela Jayawardane ensured the Lankans could restrict Pakistan to only 123/7. The Pakistanis failed to capitalize as they panicked to lose wickets early and at regular intervals. Jayawardane's decision to replace spinner Dhananjay Perera with Rangana Herath proved a masterstroke as he clinched three important wickets at a crucial stage. On this day, Shahid Afridi had scored the record fastest ODI century against the same opponents exactly 16 years ago. However, he could not repeat the magic this time around and in fact was bowled off the first ball he faced.

The Pakistani defeat means this T20 world cup will see the emergence of a new champion. The winners of the Australia–West Indies match will play the finals against Sri Lanka on Sunday. In case the Windies enter the finals, it will be the first for them whereas the hosts and Australia had already played the finals once respectively, but in vain. India, Pakistan and England who had won the cup on earlier editions respectively have returned empty handed and will certainly rue the missed opportunities.

Inspite of winning 4 out of the 5 matches played, India exited the world cup as it failed to manage a better net run rate than Pakistan. India's dismal show against the Aussies was enough to undo all their good work in the other matches and this coupled with numerous tactical errors by their skipper, like dropping Sehwag against the mighty Aussies, not playing Harbhajan against the Proteas who are not at their best against quality spinners and being non-responsive to situations cost the team dear. The captaincy has again come under the scanner, especially for the defensive field placements and not allowing the specialist bowlers to bowl their full quota when the Aussies were thrashing the part time bowlers all around.

The Kiwis lost two of their super eight matches in the super overs. Thanks to the mauling of India and South Africa, their heavy defeat against Pakistan could not stop Aussies' stride to the last four. Faced with elimination, Pakistan played their best cricket against the Kangaroos which also resulted in shutting out India's progress. The Kiwis played the semi-finals in all the previous editions and have never played a final and lost all their super eight matches this time around. A classic example of the uncertainities of T20 cricket!

CHAPTER SIXTY-ONE

ONE AND ONLY SEHWAG BIDS ADIEU

(Week ending November 07, 2015)

Virender Sehwag, the Nawab of Najafgarh recently retired from international cricket. The aggressive Indian opener will quit playing domestic cricket at the end of this season and will not feature in future IPL's as well.

Sehwag started playing for the Indian cricket team in 1999 and represented the country in 104 Tests, 251 ODIs and 19 T20Is. His two triple tons in Tests with a highest score of 319, his highest ODI score of 219 and a narrow miss of his third triple ton in Tests are proof of his immense appetite for huge scores. He is the only batsman in international cricket who went on to surpass 150 on 10 successive occasions where he achieved a Test ton. This depicts his temperament and stamina to stay in the crease.

During his illustrious career, Sehwag was part of team India which reached the 2003 World Cup final, won the ICC World T20 in 2007 and the World Cup in 2011. He has scored 8,536 runs in Tests at an average of 49.34 and 8,273 ODI runs at an average of 35.00. Gifted with supreme hand-eye co-ordination, it was his style of his play which mesmerised everyone more than his batting achievements.

Nobody came close to being the nightmare that the recently-retired Virender Sehwag was in his prime according to Dale Steyn. The bowler, whose lethal pace is intimidating for most batsmen around the world, said he always found the going tough against an on-song Sehwag.

Having scored 298 and still hitting a six is something unimaginable and you need to be a genius for that, said Waqar Younis. Sehwag's speciality has always been, reaching three figure milestones with a four or a six. Shane Warne wanted Sehwag in his team always. He loved to watch Sehwag bat, but never liked to bowl to him.

Sehwag was entertainment redefined. He always believed only in attack. Test cricket was sometimes considered to be as boring as counting shells on a sea shore. But with Sehwag's arrival, test cricket reached new dimensions. With his fearless hitting, he enthralled the fans and was capable of producing a result in a session or two.

His intentions were clear like a crystal and his mind was an open textbook. He backed his strengths and instincts, and was aggressive most of the time. He never wasted any delivery that could be swatted, as he never resorted to any defensive tactics no matter what the situation was.

No one, other than Sehwag would dare to whack the first ball of an innings for a boundary regardless of the quality of the delivery or the bowler. No one, absolutely no one will fill his shoes.

Experts criticized him for his ridiculous technique which lacked feet movement. They also urged him to control his attacking impulses. But Sehwag paid no attention to the tide of conventional dogmas, as even if earth turns upside down, he wasn't ready to change his inimitable batting style. If Sehwag's mental resilience was underestimated, so was his technique or atleast certain strands of his technique.

He also knew which bowlers to target. Aakash Chopra recalls how ruthlessly Sehwag seized on the most vulnerable bowler. He knew exactly which bowlers he could destroy. That takes intelligence as well as self-awareness. And it is a huge benefit to the team. A batsman who can knock out one of the opposition's bowlers changes the whole balance of the match. If one bowler effectively cannot bowl when Sehwag is at the wicket, then the others tire much more quickly. Sehwag's approach was never naïve or reckless, but was deeply pragmatic. He had the courage to stick to his method and the conviction that when he got back on a pitch that suited him, he would make it pay.

Dashing openers have always been with us, but nobody yet has managed to do it with the audacity and frequency of Sehwag. His figures are impressive even before you consider the thrilling manner of their compilation. Two triple and four double hundreds in a 72-Test career is a weighty achievement for one who bats as if needing to catch the last plane out of town. As most of his innings proceeded at a run-a-ball, or better, there was a high-risk element to his shot-making. And yet, there was also an appetite for runs at odds with the thrill-seeker in him that chases boundaries. When he first appeared, bowlers consoled themselves with the fact that while humiliation was always likely, it would probably be brief. His aggressive approach has revolutionised the opener's role, instead of caution and occupation of the crease, as a means of removing the new ball's shine.

There won't be another player like Sehwag. Because you would rarely find someone with such an uncluttered and uncomplicated mind, says his long time opening partner Gautam Gambhir. There won't be many who would stick to his style in times of failure. Each of his 23 Test tons and 15 ODI tons are gems and are probably with the best of strike rates. He was the only batsman who used to sing on the wicket when on a song, slightly different from the great Lawrence Rowe of West Indies who used to whistle whilst batting. Today, everyone bats for Sehwag, but batting can never be the same again without Viru!

CHAPTER SIXTY-TWO

TEAMS AIM TO END YEAR ON A HIGH

(Week ending December 22, 2012)

A big sense of relief to Team India as the Test series against England has finally come to an end, though not on expected lines. In fact, the final outcome was not as per England's expectations at the beginning of the series either. For England, winning a series in India after 27 years in a most deserving manner (2-1) is a proud moment to cherish. By winning here, England have sent a clear message to the rest of the cricketing world that with commitment and a positive attitude, beating India at home is very much possible.

The final Test at Nagpur gave illusions of a win for India for some time. But as the Test progressed, their batsmen continued to suffer in the hands of the English bowlers with James Anderson being the chief wrecker . The Indian bowlers continued to disappoint in the second innings too. The Indian skipper looked clueless with his defensive field placings and his moves clearly gave an impression India were trying to draw the match. A positive batting approach and attacking bowling in the second innings could have produced a win in India's favour.

India will now embark on the shorter formats and are sure to feel at home. They will play 2 T20's against England followed by 2 T20's and 3 ODI's against Pakistan before the year ends. England will return after Christmas for a 5 match ODI series. Having accomplished the Test series mission, England have chosen to rest their stars Trott, Anderson and Swann for the T20's. It would be better if India takes a leaf out of England's books which will ensure specialist players for different formats and full utilisation of the bench strength as well. India are currently ranked 3rd in T20's and if they win all of the upcoming four matches, they can climb to the top spot.

Australia grabbed a thrilling win against Sri Lanka in the first Test of the 3 match series. With a target of almost 400 runs, Sri Lanka found it very hard to resist the twin pace attack and survive the last day of the Test. For the next Test, Jackson Bird has replaced injured Hilfenhaus whilst Michael Clarke, for whom Usman Khwaja is brought in as cover, is struggling to overcome a hamstring injury. If Clarke remains unfit, Shane Watson is set to lead the Aussies in the Boxing Day Test. Unless the Lankans find ways to handle the Aussie pacers, the Kangaroos are set to wrap up the series.

It took four Tests for Australia to earn their first victory this summer. While Michael Clarke tightened the noose on the Lankans with an attacking field, Peter Siddle, with a career best match figures of 9 for 104 and Mitchell Starc's second best career figures of 5 for 63 ensured Australia overcame their failure to wrap up the South African innings recently.

New Zealand's current tour of South Africa will consist of 3 T20's, 2 Tests and 3 ODI's. After much controversy at home, the Kiwis will be led by Brendon McCullum and they are sure to feel the absence of former skipper Ross Taylor. For the Proteas, injured Parnell will be replaced by Ryan McLaren whilst DeVilliers has opted to rest and has withdrawn from the T20's.

CHAPTER SIXTY-THREE

TEAMS GEAR UP FOR LONG ORDEAL

(Week ending November 03, 2012)

Hosts India and visitors England are vigorously warming up for the upcoming Test series with the first Test to be played in Ahmedabad from the 15th of this month. The visitors are scheduled to play three warm-up matches as a part of their preparation process. Skipper Alistair Cook and Samit Patel began confidently in the first warm-up with a ton each. Cook and Kevin Pietersen are expected to form the backbone of the English batting with supporting roles to be played by players like Jonathan Trott, Ian Bell and Matt Prior.

For India, most of the senior players have opted to play Ranji matches with a view to regaining their dwindling form before they step in to play the first Test. Skipper Dhoni, suffering from fever is the only player who has chosen to rest as he is keen to remain fit in time for the first Test. Yuvraj Singh, Suresh Raina and Manoj Tiwary are the main contenders for the no. 6 batting slot which is up for grabs. All these three had a chance to stake claim with a good show in the first warm-up game. Though Raina failed to capitalize, Yuvraj excelled with a fine all-round display scoring a quick fire half century and grabbing a few wickets. Though Manoj Tiwary made a classy 93, he is likely to be overlooked and the selectors might opt for either Yuvraj or Raina going into the first Test.

The Indians are likely to rely on their spinners to deliver. It is not uncommon in Tests for home teams to exploit conditions to their advantage as always seen in countries like England, Australia and South Africa too. With England not able to boast of tested spinners other than Graeme Swann, the Indian batsmen are favourites to handle them confidently. On the other hand, the English men may find themselves clueless against the likes of Ashwin and Ojha and certainly have an uphill task on hand. This chink in their armour may ultimately lead to their downfall in this series if they do not find ways to overcome this. Having scored his last Test century

25 innings ago in January 2011, ageing Tendulkar will surely look forward to silent his critics with a ton or two for India.

With cyclone in the area, the one-off T20 between hosts Sri Lanka and New Zealand was abandoned halfway as expected and they will now play a five match ODI series. West Indies are also set to play hosts Bangladesh in a two Test series. England, New Zealand and the West Indies are faced with common problems when it comes to handling spinners in the sub-continent.

Down under, the Aussies seem to be planning well for the first Test against South Africa. They have been systematic in their selection process and are clear with their strategy. Moves like recalling Shane Watson from CLT20, opting to pick Matthew Wade ahead of out of form Brad Haddin as their first choice keeper, sitting out Pat Cummins as he hasn't played first class cricket for over a year, etc., are certainly smart moves. They have opted for a four pronged pace attack and have given opener Ed Cowan yet another chance to cement his position.

It's now time for international cricketers to play for national pride!

CHAPTER SIXTY-FOUR

TEST CRICKET RECORDS UNIQUE RECORDS

(Week ending November 08, 2012)

The week belonged to Abul Hassan, Bangladesh's rookie medium-pacer. Surprisingly, it is not for his bowling efforts, but for his scintillating century (113) against the West Indies in the second Test on debut, that too batting at no.10. In the process, he created history for Bangladesh by becoming only the second no.10 batsman to have scored a century on debut in 135 years of Test cricket. The first one to accomplish this was Australia's Reggie Duff way back in 1902 against England at home in Melbourne, but in the second innings. It will probably take a number of decades for this feat to be repeated.

The centuries spree of the previous week ended with Cheteshwar Pujara's maiden double hundred for India and English skipper Alastair Cook's heroic 176 in the second innings which went in vain and enabled India to wrap up the match on the fifth day as expected. With his double ton, Pujara has shown glimpses of getting into Rahul Dravid's shoes in the near future for his team and might probably end up the next wall of India. From the rival camp, Cook played the innings of his lifetime in a losing cause and showed everyone why his batting is held in high regard.

With a comeback century after a long time, Virender Sehwag is set to become the ninth Indian cricketer to play 100 Tests, come second Test. His average of 50.89 and strike rate of 82.45 (best in Test cricket) alongwith his 23 centuries and 32 fifties place him on a high pedestal. He is the only Indian and the fourth in the world to score a triple century twice. In fact, the third triple was for the taking when he blew it away by gifting his wicket to Muralitharan whilst on 294. Inspite of this, his ardent fans believe it is only a matter of time before he repeats this feat. He also holds the unique record of crossing 150 on 14 occasions, 10 of them on the trot, ie., whenever he scored a 100.

Australia and South Africa are playing the second Test and it is a repeat story. The hosts lost 3 early wickets, including that of clueless Ponting yet again. Michael Clarke created Test history by scoring a double century again, his fourth for the year. In the process, he became the first Test batsman to have achieved this, leaving behind Don Bradman and Ricky Ponting. With David Warner scoring a century earlier in the day, it was left to Clarke and Mike Hussey to score back to back double hundred and hundred respectively. Nothing, including the short pitched stuff from the Proteas, seemed to unsettle Michael Clarke who is on a dream run.

South Africa lost Philander before the toss due to a back problem and suffered further blows when Jacques Kallis and Dale Steyn left the field midway due to harmstring injuries. While Steyn is back on the field, Kallis' injury looks more serious and he is not likely to bowl again in the match. With Imran Tahir not making any impact, it seems the Proteas' woes are set to continue throughout the series. The Aussies scored 482 for 5 on day one, probably yet another record in Test history and this summarises the visitors' plight!

CHAPTER SIXTY-FIVE

TEST GIANTS BATTLE FOR SUPREMACY

(Week ending November 08, 2012)

The week saw yet another feather added to Sachin Tendulkar's cap when he was conferred with the Order of Australia for his role in promoting India-Australia relations through sport. He is the second Indian and fourth non-Australian cricketer after Sir Garyfield Sobers, Clive Lloyd and Brian Lara, all West Indians, to receive this honour.

This week will be one of the most interesting weeks for Test cricket. The current no.1 and three former no.1 ranks will be seen in action in two separate series which are set to be cliff hangers. While the Kangaroos-Proteas series is set to be a battle of pace batteries, the India –England series is expected to be dominated by Indian spinners. When the Aussies visited South Africa in 2009 and defended their no.1 status, the Proteas were far away from achieving this milestone. Since then, these two have played each other in 3 series and are locked 4-4. Australia, thanks to the Ashes debacle after the 2009 Proteas tour, have slid down the rankings and will be going into this series as underdogs, first time ever in a home series.

Australia, India and England have all held the no.1 Test ranking in the recent years and a win for Australia over South Africa will see them get back to the hot seat. England lost it at home against the Proteas and India lost it in England against the hosts. With four Tests slated to be played at home, this will be the best chance for India to march towards regaining the top spot with a home series against Aussies to follow. South Africa will be full of confidence going into this series. The last Proteas won two successive Tests was in Perth and Melbourne in 2008 and they haven't won two in a row in their past 20 matches. Whereas Australia, after winning 8 out of their last 10 Tests, have risen from the nadir and they will never have a better chance than now to regain the no.1 spot.

England have always been troubled by spin in the sub-continent other than against Bangladesh. With three specialist spinners in the squad, India certainly have a big advantage and their skipper Dhoni will surely nurture high expectations from them. England last won a major series in the sub-continent in 2000-01 against Sri Lanka and only supreme confidence and committed performance will ensure the jinx is broken this time.

Though England's batting is strengthened by their skipper Alistair Cook and Kevin Pietersen, they seem to be suffering in their bowling front. Already Steven Finn and Stuart Broad with a thigh injury and bruised heel respectively are doubtful starters for the first Test. Their ace spinner Graeme Swann is back in England to spend time with his daughter who is unwell, but will be back for the Ahmedabad Test. England have already flown in Surrey fast bowler Stuart Meaker as a back-up for Finn.

One positive sign for England is that they have a solid bench strength with players like Eoin Morgan, Johnny Bairstow, Nick Compton, Samit Patel and Joe Root putting up their hands! For India, though Laxman and Dravid will be missing, Tendulkar, Sehwag and Gambhir are expected to inspire the younger batsmen with their batting heroics!

CHAPTER SIXTY-SIX

TESTING WEEK FOR TEST TEAMS

(Week ending March 16, 2013)

Four Tests are being played simultaneously this week. Considering the excessive amount of shorter format games being played nowadays, this is indeed very rare in the annals of Test cricket. The only two teams not playing Test cricket this week, Pakistan and South Africa are locked in a 5 match ODI series with hosts Proteas leading 1-0. They seem to be carrying their recent Test form forward and look likely to dominate the ODI series inspite of their recent lone T20 humiliation in the hands of Pakistan.

The drawn first Test between Sri Lanka and Bangladesh at Galle saw history repeated with eight hundreds being scored. The first time was during the West Indies – South Africa Test match at St. John's in 2005 when 4 from each side scored tons. The current match saw Sangakkara coming from a long injury lay off scoring two hundreds. While Ashraful missed a double century narrowly, Mushfiqur went on to score a double, the first ever by a Bangladeshi batsman in Tests. Only 18 wickets fell while 1,543 runs were scored during the match.

England's Nick Compton recorded his second successive century of the series and Jonathan Trott also chipped in with one on the first day of the second Test. Having let off England in the first Test, it seems New Zealand are now finding it extremely hard to run through this English batting line-up. It is surprising to see how a couple of confident knocks by England have transformed the Kiwis, making them appear toothless on home conditions. With the pitch not providing much assistance and England's bowlers struggling to run through teams in the tour so far, New Zealand are still in with a chance to manage to draw this Test.

After getting mauled in the first two Tests, Australia are compounded with problems from within well before the third Test has even begun. Their vice-captain Shane Watson has returned home after being axed alongwith Pattinson, Khawaja and Mitchell Johnson from the third Test playing eleven.

Off-field disciplinary issues and problems with attitude seem to have taken their toll whilst form or lack of it had nothing to do with it.

Brad Haddin, flown in from Australia for injured Matthew Wade has been named in the playing XI alongwith off-spinner Lyon and all-rounder Steven Smith. The visitors have chosen to go in with a three pronged pace and a dual spin attack with Maxwell sitting out. For India, post Sehwag's axing, Shikar Dhawan is set to make his Test debut and looking into his recent form and achievements, it looks like he will surely capitalise. With Pujara too overcoming an injury scare, India look to maintain their unbeaten record in Mohali and are on the verge of their biggest series win over Aussies. India has till date, never had more than 2 wins in a series victory over the Aussies.

After getting thoroughly thrashed in the ODI and T20 series in the West Indies, Zimbabwe are fighting hard in the ongoing Test series. Inspite of posting a low first innings total of 211, they have not allowed the hosts to run away with a big lead. Zimbabwe's bowling has been a revelation so far and their batsmen need to match them to win the series.

CHAPTER SIXTY-SEVEN

TRIPLE CROWN FOR SOUTH AFRICA

(Week ending September 01, 2012)

India U19 deservedly lifted the world cup by beating the hosts and favourites, Australia last Sunday. The match was dominated by the skippers of both sides with India emerging eventual winners, thanks to Unmukt's unbeaten 100.

Both the teams peaked at the right time coming into the finals. If India beat Pakistan in a cliff-hanger quarterfinal, Australia overcame a few hiccups earlier when they beat Bangladesh. Inspite of losing the opening match to the West Indies, India, helped by timely and vital contributions from most of the players, grew in confidence as the tournament progressed, especially after the triumph over Pakistan which could have ended in a literal hara-kari for India.

India has now won the world cup three times and has equalled Australia. For India, inspite of his personal contributions, the skipper let his boys do the talking.

Players like Aparajith, Harmeet and Sanjeev Sharma ensured matters never got out of hand. Sanjeev Sharma deserves special praise for his early and vital breakthroughs in all the matches he played. A few of these, alongwith Unmukt, are sure to play for the senior team and make a mark in the years to come.

The two Test series between India and the Kiwis is turning out to be a one sided affair as expected. The Kiwi's inability to play quality spinners was exposed once again after their recent debacle in the Caribbean.

The second Test at Bengaluru should produce a similiar result ending in a 2-0 series win to the hosts. Cheteshwar Pujara's ton in the first Test should enable him cement his place in the team atleast for this year.

The week also saw the English skipper Strauss throw a bombshell by deciding to quit all forms of competitive cricket with immediate effect. Inspite of taking England to the top spot in Test rankings, Strauss felt he has ran his race following the recent 0-2 loss to the Proteas which saw his team dethroned. With this, yet another gentleman cricketer will be missed.

He played exactly 100 Tests and 124 ODI's for his team. His record 21 Test centuries and 6 ODI hundreds clearly indicate he is more of Test class and his contributions spread over his 10 year career will always be remembered. Whatever the reasons, England have now lost two of their stalwarts ever since the recent SMS episode of Kevin Pietersen.

The current week also saw South Africa on top of all the three formats of the game. This came after they beat England comprehensively by 80 runs in the second ODI. Known to be chokers for a long time, they are now rewarded for their untiring efforts over the years.

Surely, they have been the team playing most consistently in the last year or so and it looks like the presence of Gary Kirsten is doing wonders to their team. This triple is an outstanding achievement, the first of it's kind!

It is currently short format matches galore. India will soon play 2 T20 matches against the Kiwis. Aussies are playing a 5 ODI and 3 T20 series against Pakistan, having already won the first match and England are currently locked in a 5 ODI cum 3 T20 series as well against the Proteas.

The next stop is the T20 world cup!

CHAPTER SIXTY-EIGHT

TURBULENT TIMES AWAIT ENGLAND

(Week ending October 27, 2012)

The Champions League T20 2012 is drawing to a close. With this, the T20 festivities will subside sans the few T20 internationals to be played during the remaining couple of months in the year. The four most deserving teams have made it to the semi-finals. As expected, Delhi Daredevils is the only IPL team to remain in the fray at this stage. Full marks to the two South African teams, Titans and Highveld Lions who have made full use of the home conditions and Sydney Sixers of Australia who exploited the familiar conditions far away from home.

Whilst Group B saw the two qualifiers decided well in advance, thanks to CSK and MI putting up a more than pathetic show, Group A extended the uncertainity to semi-finals aspirants till the last day of the group stage. All Auckland Aces had to do was to win their last encounter against Perth Scorchers and wait for a favourable result from the next match between Delhi and Titans which was subsequently washed out. They choked here to stumble and fall whilst chasing a meagre target. A decent win would have seen them through.

International cricket is set to return in November with a bang. The playing formats are set to grow longer as they days progress. While Australia will host the Proteas in a three Test series, Sri Lanka will play 1 T20, 5 ODI's and 2 Test matches against New Zealand at home. As a result of Mahela Jayawardane quitting his T20 captaincy, Angelo Mathews will lead them in T20's for the next one year and Lasith Malinga will be his deputy. The series between Australia and South Africa is set to keep cricket fans world over on their toes and the Proteas' fans at home awake the whole night as the matches will begin well past midnight South African time.

Indian players will finally return to Test cricket after a long hiatus after a few hectic months of T20 cricket. Their home series against England will be for over 3 months and will involve 4 Tests, 2 T20's and 5 ODI's. The English players will visit home for Christmas and return in January 2012 to play the ODI leg and complete the series commitments. India, though will miss Rahul Dravid and VVS Laxman, will be charged up to avenge their recent Test battering on the English soil. Kevin Pietersen's timely return is a big boost and a shot in the arm for England. Their success hinges on how well they handle Indian spinners as well as Pietersen.

India's decision to leave out spinners in the India A team for the visitors' first warm up match has been severely criticised by former England captain Michael Vaughan and a few others. Vaughan feels this is a pathetic decision and is quite far from the spirit of the game whereas BCCI sees nothing abnormal in this. England is expected to grapple with spin friendly tracks and tackle atleast a couple of spinners in each of their matches. This move will deprive them of the much needed exposure and acclimatization to spinners in the Indian conditions.

For England's Matt Prior, beating India in India is their biggest challenge, much bigger than their triumph over Australia over the years. They last did it in 1985!

CHAPTER SIXTY-NINE

TV STING TESTING CRICKET YET AGAIN

(Week ending May 19, 2012)

It was great to see the red cherry and white clothing on the cricket field again after quite some time, thanks to the just begun England-West Indies Test series after an overdose of T20 cricket, courtesy IPL 5 with all the off-field drama associated with it. The first Test will also see the debutant Jonathan Bairstow, the son of former England wicket-keeper David Bairstow in action, thanks to the injury sustained by Ravi Bopara.

The first day of the three Test series saw the usual collapse of the Windies batting with Chanderpaul standing tall amidst their dismal batting performance on a batting friendly day one. Chanderpaul who became the 10th batsman to cross 10,000 Test runs just a month ago continued with his run scoring spree in style yet again. It is scary to imagine this Windies batting line-up sans Chanderpaul, but for whose consistently stubborn batting, his team would have probably never touched the three figure mark in the last couple of months in any of their outings. The youngsters let the team down again and looking from the confident spells of Jimmy Anderson and Stuart Broad, it looks like England are very keen to make a dominant start to this series.

Ever since the West Indies beat England in the 2009 Jamaica Test, they have played 30 Tests between them and the Windies have won only two of them till date. The English skipper Andrew Strauss who has failed to score a century in his last 49 Test innings coming into this Test must surely be run hungry and waiting to get back into scoring ways and will not miss this opportunity to score a century or two. Unless the visitors step up their game and play attacking cricket, they do not stand any chance of overwhelming the reigning no.1 Test team in seam-friendly conditions.

With the IPL entering the last week, Delhi Daredevils are deservedly leading the table with Kolkata Knight Riders closely following them. Punjab Kings XI have kept their chances alive with a smart win over reigning champions Chennai Super Kings and thereby pushing them to the brink of elimination. The next couple of days will decide the last four. The last two spots are still open with four teams still in with a chance. The teams to watch out will be Delhi Daredevils and Royal Challengers Bangalore.

Chris Gayle became the first to score three centuries in IPL and has also hit more than 50 sixers in this IPL. His unbeaten 128 against Delhi in 62 balls with 13 sixers has a strong message written all over it, "Get me and the cup is yours"!

A recent TV sting operation in India has exposed corruption of the highest order in cricket yet again. While the whole world was believing that the fixing virus in cricket was eradicated ever since the Pakistani trio's recent involvement was exposed and they were thoroughly punished, the fixing monster has reared it's head yet again. With the enormous amount of money the IPL has been generating, it was prone to this ugly situation in each of it's early editions as well. It is sad that cricket, once deemed to be a gentleman's game, is now under scrutiny and is waging a battle to retain it's declining glory.

Five players, all budding Indian domestic cricketers who are believed to have fallen prey and succumbed to the money bait have been placed under a 15 day suspension, pending inquiry. They will not able to take part in any form of cricket. This time, the needle is pointing not only to the players, but to the franchisees as well. This is probably the first ever instance in cricket where allegations of fixing by players and black money payments by franchisees have come out together. Though the BCCI was quick enough to act on players, their continued inaction on misdeeds by franchisees remains a mystery raising fears that probably the culprits are being selectively protected by the apex body of cricket.

One positive development is the instant involvement of the Government Of India in addressing this menace with the demands increasing for a parliamentary probe and the Union Sports Minister suggesting the BCCI go into the root cause of this and come out with long term solutions including distancing itself from IPL in future, a la English Premiership style.

As if this drama was not enough, it was sad to see Shah Rukh Khan, the leading Bollywood icon and owner of Kolkata Knight Riders getting involved in a post match brawl at Wankhede Stadium with the state cricket officials. With accusations and counter accusations flying around, the star is facing a probable life ban from entering this renowned stadium.

Stings may give cricket testing times, but the game will stand the test of time!

CHAPTER SEVENTY

VISITING TEAMS DOMINATE SUB-CONTINENT

(Week ending December 01, 2012)

The results of three matches played simultaneously during the week went in favour of the visiting teams while hosts Australia failed to seal a certain win in the fourth. This is indeed a rare happening and raises the question whether the visitors are gaining confidence in alien conditions or the hosts are crumbling under intense pressure from fans and local admirers. The only match which produced no result saw South Africa play admirable cricket to escape from the jaws of defeat with an honourable draw.

In Sri Lanka, the Kiwis overcame five consecutive defeats in the recent past to carve out a fine win in the second Test against the hosts. Their skipper Ross Taylor showed the way with a fine century and deservedly won the man of the match award. In the bowling front, it was Tim Southee who steered the demolition job. The first Test saw New Zealand getting mauled within three days. What unfolded in the second was a magnificient comeback resulting in a historic series leveling win. The 167 run win is incidentally identical to the Kiwis' previous victory here way back in 1998.

In Bangladesh, the West Indies won both the Tests against the hosts convincingly. Inspite of the games producing tall scores, it was the visitors' fiery bowling which made all the difference and surprisingly the men in form, Chris Gayle in the batting and Sunil Naraine in the bowling fronts failed respectively. The two teams now go into the five match ODI series and Bangladesh have already been jolted with the absence of their world no.1 ODI all-rounder Shakib Al Hasan due to a shin injury which will have a big impact on Bangladesh's chances.

India got their worst home drubbing in recent times when they lost to England in Mumbai, their seventh home defeat in this millennium. What was embarrassing was they lost by ten wickets and that too, in less than four days. The selectors overlooked the dismal performance of the entire team and retained the same team. Surprisingly, instead of declaring teams for the remaining Tests and two T'20's as announced earlier, they picked a team only for the Kolkata Test. Have the selectors compromised on the result of the series or have persisted with the current team just to give a final chance to the players to either perform or perish?

With the series level at 0-0, the third and final Test between Australia and South Africa at Perth is set to be a sell out thriller. Thanks to the Proteas managing to draw the previous Test, a draw or win in the final Test, which will be their 200th, will retain them in the top rank whereas the Aussies can regain the top spot with a win in the final Test. Such is the importance of injured Jacques Kallis to the team, that his captain is desperate to play him atleast as a pure batsman.

Former Aussie skipper Ricky Ponting will be playing his 168th and last Test at Perth. He bid adieu to international cricket after getting convinced he isn't making any contributions to his team. He had a chequered career and was Aussies' best captain ever and their most prolific run scorer. He and his captivating presence will always be missed on field!

CHAPTER SEVENTY-ONE

VISITORS STRUGGLE IN ALIEN CONDITIONS

(Week ending March 02, 2013)

Four international cricket matches were played during the week and the hosts excelled in three of them leaving the visitors perplexed with England being the only exception when they beat hosts New Zealand in the third and deciding ODI to clinch the series 2-1. It was fascinating to see the English bowlers rise to the occasion when it mattered the most to ensure they gifted their coach Andy Flower with a well deserved ODI series win abroad. For New Zealand, skipper Brendon McCullum yet again scored a belligerent 79, but in a losing cause. Losing Guptill to injury seems to have cost the Kiwis the series as he too was in prime form. The teams will now clash in a 3 Test series.

The ODI series between the West Indies and Zimbabwe finished on expected lines in a 3-0 sweep by the hosts, Windies. Zimbabwe has a long way to go as far as their team standard is concerned and it seems lack of sufficient match exposure is also affecting them and eroding their confidence level substantially. Former skipper Ramnaresh Sarwan justified his inclusion with a hundred in the second ODI, thanks to a major reprive from the umpire and the visitors not going for the DRS option. West Indies won all their matches convincingly and the teams will now play 2 T20's and 2 Tests respectively.

Pakistan's lost the third Test by an innings and 18 runs. There was not even one fifty from the Pakistan batsmen in this Test and no batsman aggregated 200 runs in the series inspite of two centurions in the second Test. The hosts have been in superb touch throughout this summer. They have played 5 Tests and have won all, 3 of them inning wins. Not even one of these matches went into the fifth day, reaffirming their bowlers' supremacy on these fast and bouncy tracks. With this series win, they have left the second placed England way behind with a 10 point lead and remain the most deserved no.1 Test team in the recent years.

For Pakistan, this is the fourth whitewash since 2000 in a series of 3 or more Tests, three of them in the hands of Australia. Thanks to Morne Morkel's injury, Kyle Abbott made his debut for the Proteas and a dream debut it was, with a match haul of 9 for 68 with 6 of them coming in the first essay. With his consistent and stupendous performance throughout the series, Dale Steyn became the third highest wicket taker for South Africa, surpassing Allan Donald with only Shaun Pollock and Makhaya Ntini ahead. The teams will now play 2 T20's and 5 ODI's respectively.

It was India all the way in the first Test against Australia. The visitors won the toss but the hosts won the match comprehensively. Aussie skipper Clarke scored a ton but Indian skipper Dhoni responded with a match turning double ton. India played with three spinners in Harbhajan Singh's 100th Test and Ashwin led the wicket riot with a career best 12 wicket haul. Glimpses of vintage Tendulkar were seen yet again. For Australia, debutant Henriques repeated Bruce Reid's debut performance with a fifty in each innings. For Aussies to win the series from here, they need to turn a new leaf!

CHAPTER SEVENTY-TWO

WINDIES KEEP THEIR WORD IN STYLE

(Week ending October 13, 2012)

When the T20 world cup started, all the eight ICC member countries had equal chances of lifting the cup. But there was one team, the West Indies, whom everyone feared silently. The final result confirmed their fears. Starting from the first round, the Windies' journey had been a ruthless one with surgical precision all through. They proved to be the most balanced team with ample firepower in their batting which is a must in this form of cricket.

Having 7 batsmen in the team as India tried and failed is just not enough. A teams needs to have sure match winners in them. As seen in the finals, getting Chris Gayle early was not everything. It was only a first step in attempting to breach the Windies' impregnable wall. Inspite of the record lowest score of only 14 in the power play, with the openers back in the dressing room, Marlon Samuels produced a peach of an innings hitherto never seen in a T20 world cup. By the 10th over, the cup was clearly in the Lankans' pocket. Samuels seized the moment to demolish the Lankan bowlers, especially their most feared strike bowler Malinga who ended up with a forgettable T20 spell.

Chris Gayle was not wrong when he boasted of a Windies' win in the finals. So high was their confidence that the moment they crossed the 130 mark, it was always an uphill task for the hosts to reach the target, especially with Sunil Naraine and Badree who not only matched the Lankan spinners, but took their bowling a notch higher. Dilshan succumbing early did not help the Lankans' cause either and they could never recover. Instead of setting right a miserable finals record, the Lankan skipper quit his captaincy.

The Windies bowled and fielded like a pack of hungry lions after man of the match Samuels gave them a new lease of life. It was evident they were on a mission and on a roll and their body language went back into the 70's and 80's when they completely dominated the cricketing world. The giant strides they took all along and in the finals culminated with the victory lap and the now famous Gangnam style dance steps much to everyone's delight and announced their arrival in style.

The T20 fever is not over yet. The Champions League 2012 is set to begin in South Africa today. The past week saw qualifying matches being played for the two available slots. Each group with three teams saw Auckland Aces and Yorkshire qualify from their respective groups. The main tournament will see two groups of 5 teams each vying for the cup. The current holders are Mumbai Indians, but surprisingly they are yet to win a IPL edition.

With T20 league teams from most of the main cricketing nations playing, the biggest contingent is from the Indian Premier League with four teams viz., Chennai, Delhi, Kolkata and Mumbai. Indian fans will be delighted to see their own teams play against each other. The South African grounds will produce a close contest between the bat and the ball unlike those in the sub-continent where batsmen dominate and grab the honours. This will make the tournament a very interest one and yet again, there will be no favourites.

CHAPTER SEVENTY-THREE

WINDIES STUMBLE AND ENGLAND FUMBLE

(Week ending March 31, 2012)

Kieron Pollard's blitzkrieg in the 4th ODI to set up an emphatic win for the West Indies giving them a 2-1 lead going into the last match and skipper Sammy's brutal assault in the last ODI went in vain as the hosts stumbled against the Aussies in their final hurdle. This meant they failed to create history of winning an ODI series against the Aussies for the first time in 16 years. Having lost the first ODI, the Windies came back strongly in the second to level the series before a last over needless run out from them saw the third match ending in an unexpected tie. This probably was the cause for the series ending in a 2-2 draw and thereby giving the Aussies renewed confidence to win the first of the two T20 games. The Aussies may have gained in confidence, but the ensuing Test series promises to be a keenly fought contest.

Back in the sub-continent, England fumbled yet again against quality spin bowling. Inspite of Jonathan Trott's fighting century, England lost their fourth Test on the trot, having lost the last three against Pakistan prior to this. The first Test of the two Test series against Sri Lanka ended in yet another loss for England in the sub-continent. This, inspite of a dream start for England in the first session of day one. Skipper Mahela Jayawardene stood tall amidst ruins to show why he is still one of the best in the business . His epic 180 ensured Lanka posted a competitive total of 318 against odds. This was enough to give his team a sizeable first innings lead and as a result, the second innings mediocre batting performance by the hosts did not affect their prospects in any way. England, set a target of 340, began promisingly with vital partnerships. It is a pity their batsmen proved yet again that handling spin is not their cup of tea. From 231 for 4 at tea, they threw away their last 6 wickets for just 31 runs. For the Lankans, Jayawardane and man of the match Rangana Herath with 6 wickets apiece in each innings were the heroes in batting and bowling respectively. England losing 18 of their 20 wickets to spin is a testimony of their fragility against spin. For the Lankans, this win is their first at home since July 2010 ever since Muralitharan retired from Test cricket.

Inspite of dominating throughout the tour and in the Test series, South Africa let New Zealand off the hook in the third Test to be content with a 1-0 series win. Kane Williamson's century for the Kiwis was very much similar to that of Trott for England against Sri Lanka. While both centuries were equally defiant, Williamson's ton earned his team an unexpected draw whereas Trott's earned his team an unexpected loss. South Africa would have returned home with ample confidence as they are certainly closing in on the no. 1 Test rank aided by England's repeated loses in Tests being played in conditions not conducive to either their batsmen or bowlers.

The Proteas are set to play India in a one off T20 match immediately on their return from New Zealand. This match is to celebrate the 150th year of Indian settlement in South Africa and this will be an annual affair henceforth. Unlike the BCCI which never believes in providing rest to their players who play round the year, the South African Board has rested most of their players for this match from the touring squad, as they are set to return home just a day before the match. This shows players' welfare is their top priority and no wonder the Proteas have performed consistently well, even while playing under different conditions.

The Indian squad will return home after this match just in time for IPL 5. The whole country is getting ready to watch this extravaganza of two months. It is sad IPL 5 will not see India's world cup hero, ailing Yuvraj Singh in action. His absence has also paved way for ex-Indian and KKR skipper Sourav Ganguly to be elected skipper-cum-mentor of Pune Warriors. Whilst Deccan Chargers have lost Ishant Sharma to an ankle injury, Jessy Ryder, inspite of recently taking an indefinite break from cricket is expected to overcome his drinking problems and play for Pune Warriors with the help of his psychologist. This IPL will also see Aussie skipper Michael Clarke and Bangladeshi Asia Cup hero Tamim Iqbal in action for the first time, both playing for Pune Warriors

Chennai Super Kings will take on Mumbai Indians in the opening match at Chennai and for the next two months, every home in India will be looking forward to early evenings, anticipating action packed drama every evening!

CHAPTER SEVENTY-FOUR

YOUNG GUNS TAKE CENTRE STAGE

(Week ending August 18, 2012)

Having lost the first match of the 3 Test series, England's back was to the wall when they began the third Test. This game is a must win for the hosts to retain their no.1 Test slot. But the last few days threw unexpected challenges to the team management in the form of Kevin Pietersen. The England Cricket Board was dealing with an issue much bigger than the game which incidentally was the creation of their man Friday, Pietersen, in the drawn second Test. Exactly at the time of strategizing to win the third Test, England's priority shifted to making a more important decision concerning the team and it's unity. This resulted in Kevin Pietersen not being picked for the all important match.

This Test will also go down in the history as the 100th Test for England's gentleman skipper Andrew Strauss, only the 9th Englishman to achieve this feat. Will he bring out something special yet again? Knowing Strauss well, he might produce a classic as only he knows the efforts and commitment his boys put in in the last one year to reach the top and he will never let this honour slip away easily. Already, inspite of choosing to bat, the Proteas have not had the best start to this Test with all their top order batsmen back in the pavilion before Tea on day one. However, with lot of cricket yet to be played, this match has a lot of action in store and is set to go to the wire.

Most of the countries playing in the forthcoming T20 world cup in Sri Lanka have named their squad, just in time before the August 18 deadline. Australia have shown faith in their 41year old veteran Brad Hogg and also picked uncapped Glenn Maxwell, while Bangladesh have recalled Mohammed Reza at the cost of Nazmul. For New Zealand, young fast bowler Adam Milne was a surprise inclusion, similar to the surprise berth Harbhajan Singh earned in the Indian squad.

Pakistan have decided to rest their veterans Younis Khan and Umar Gul for the ODI series to be played against Australia at the UAE. It now looks like curtains to Younis Khan's one day career. It seems the selectors are not only unhappy with his recent form and poor performance, but are also surprised at his extremely slow pace of batting in the shorter format. In his chequered career, Younis has piled up 6,824 runs from 245 innings at an average of 32.18. However, his last 10 innings have produced just 97 runs inspite of one half century.

Down under in Australia, budding cricketers, some of them future heroes for their respective nations, are fighting out for the U-19 world cup. The teams are divided into 4 groups of 4 teams each. Expectedly, Australia, England, Pakistan, New Zealand, West Indies, India and South Africa have made it to the quarter-finals from their respective groups. Surprisingly, Sri Lanka failed to make it to the last eight and this slot was deservedly grabbed by Bangladesh coming from the same group.

The quarter final to watch out for will be the one between arch rivals India and Pakistan. The young guns playing in this world cup have been displaying exemplary fighting spirt in the battle for supremacy!

CHAPTER SEVENTY-FIVE

CHAMPIONS SLIDE, BUT TURN OUT A CHAMPION SIDE

(Week ending March 03, 2012)

After losing their last league game against the Aussies, even the Indian skipper was of the view his team has forfeited all the chances of making it to the CB Series finals. Looking into Team India's lack of form as well as confidence, it was highly unlikely they will even beat the Sri Lankans, leave alone managing the bonus point to keep their chances alive in the competition. Tuesday was a special day in the history of ODI cricket as India pulled off a miraculous quickfire chase to pull the carpet from under the Lankans' feet. As mentioned earlier, cricket is indeed a funny game with innumerable twists and turns. If every moment was awkward for the Indians so far in this tour, everything was right with their run chase as it appeared their batsmen have woken up from deep slumber. With India nearing victory even much before the required 40 over mark in order to earn the bonus point, their fortunes changed dramatically and their body language totally transformed in the middle.

Being on the brink of elimination, the batsmen, for the first time in the whole tour, got their act together for India. If the openers gave a more than a brisk start, Gambhir and Raina rallied around Virat Kohli beautifully to script only the second most popular run chases in the ODI history closely following the magnificient chase of 435 by the Proteas against the Aussies a few years ago. It was great to see Kohli, on whose shoulders the country's future prospects wrest, bat with utmost ease which also ensured they did not require their ever reliable finisher, Dhoni, to bat. His stroke play was so audacious that Lasith Malinga, the Lankan sling bowler who is a terror in ODI cricket had to suffer the ignonimity of ending up with the worst analysis (96 runs off 7.4 overs) in ODI cricket ever in a 8 over spell. The two controversial decisions against them in their previous match against the Aussies look to have spurred the Indians on. It was also sad to see magnificient centuries by Dilshan and Sangakkara respectively going in vain. Dilshan must be dejected to see his score of 160, the second against the Indians in an ODI, also going in vain. At the halfway stage, with the Lankans making a mammoth 320, they seemed to have one foot already in the final. But India clearly had other ideas.

One look at Kohli's stupendous effort in this match and his various consistently vital knocks throughout this tour make him deservedly the only batsman from the Indian camp to have scored a century each in the Test series as well as the current ODI competition. Inspite of mediocre bowling by the Indians, Kohli's 133 n.o. of just 86 balls ensured India now have a stronger chance of entering the finals at the expense of the Lankans. With consistent losses after leading the points table and looking into the other two teams' consistent form, India never stood a chance of making it to the finals. But they had an ace up their sleeve in Kohli and pulled out their trump card in their last encounter of the league phase to keep their chances alive. India have done it's part in style and now their fortune is in the Aussies' hands who need to beat the Lankans for India to qualify.

Sri Lanka's mediocre bowling, sloppy fielding, delaying of taking bowling powerplay and inability to contain the Indian openers might have eased the Indians' run chase, but this will certainly take nothing away from the Indian batsmen. With Kohli taking Malinga to the cleaners, the rest of the bowlers, were all at sea. This led to the Lankans' caving in after three magnificient straight wins in the tournament.

It is great to see Kohli come in not only with excellent skills but with lots of self-belief as well. It is remarkable to see him stand up for his team when the world cup hero Yuvraj Singh is confined to his treatment and seniors are grappling with their form. The feature of this historic chase, simply put, has been that India was never lagging behind in the asking rate, inspite of going without a boundary for 35 deliveries at one stage. It was heartening to see the champions slide down the points table, but they did show for once, they are a champion side by earning themselves a life-line!

In the other news of the week, both England and South Africa clinched the T20 as well as the ODI series against their rivals Pakistan and New Zealand respectively. Let us hope the Kiwis bounce back atleast in the forthcoming Test series and keep the tradition of home wins alive.

www.ingramcontent.com/pod-product-compliance
Lightning Source LLC
LaVergne TN
LVHW091321150826
845673LV00006B/1726

* 9 7 9 8 8 9 3 2 2 0 9 2 6 *